STILL LC

Still Love Left

Faith and Hope in Later Life

Michael Jackson

YOUCAXTON
PUBLICATIONS

ISBN 978-1-913425-68-5
Published by YouCaxton Publications 2021
YCBN: 01

YouCaxton Publications
www.youcaxton.co.uk

You are confronted with yourself. Each year
The pouches fill, the skin is uglier.
You give it all unflinchingly. You stare
Into yourself, beyond. Your brush's care
Runs with self-knowledge. Here
Is a humility at one with craft.
There is no arrogance. Pride is apart
From this self-scrutiny. You make light drift
The way you want. Your face is bruised and hurt
But there is still love left.

From Rembrandt's Late Self-Portraits by Elizabeth Jennings

This book is dedicated to the memory of my parents Ian and Cynthia who had to negotiate old age in different ways but whose lives together moulded me in ways for which I shall always be grateful, and who certainly taught me that there is always love left.

Contents

FOREWORD

Old age can be a time of great surprise. But, there are popular conceptions in the western world that suggest something different. Old age is seen as a problem - a time of decline and increasing dependency. The failing of faculties or the diminishing of physical powers come to characterise a time of life that in other cultures is respected or even revered. And the surprise?

Christians are familiar with writings that constantly surprise. One of them comes early in the Old Testament narrative when two nomads, Abram and his wife Sarai, reach old age without a child. Given that 'blessing' involved seeding future generations - and Abram had been promised that he would be a blessing to all the nations - this was turning into a bit of a joke. Yet, old age turned out to hold a few unexpected turns. When Sarai found out she was to give birth, she laughed; her husband had no idea how to cope.

This isn't the only example. Ageing is seen as the cumulation of a life of experience and learning, a source of hard-won wisdom, a gift that should be honoured by those who themselves will one day be old. Age as a gift to be prized.

Michael Jackson has experienced caring for elderly people, and explored both theological meaning and pastoral understanding. In his personal experience of family relationships and his professional life in the charitable sector and pastoral ministry he has thought deeply about the impact and significance of ageing. In this beautifully written book he opens the reader to the beauty and possibilities of age. With a depth that he bears lightly, he reflects on dignity, love and faith.

This is a book that should be widely read and shared. Michael Jackson describes human mortality - the acceptance of which can be seen to be the beginning of freedom - with realism, hope and reverence. He does so with acceptance and even joy. And he shines a different light on a process of human growth that restores to old age the substance it deserves. He challenges some of the popular misconceptions and looks differently at what many of us will one day experience for ourselves. And he does this with a generous and uncomplicated spirit. It is a beautiful book.

The Right Reverend Nicholas Baines
Bishop of Leeds
May 2020

PREFACE

It may be helpful to give some perspective on how this book came to be written. After twenty five years as Director of St. John's Winchester Charity, the Trustees of the Charity kindly gave me a sabbatical during which I had the chance to reflect on many of the issues explored here, and the book began to take shape in my mind. Now known as St. John's Charity, the charity is a unique Christian foundation. Founded as a medieval hospital supporting the poor and needy of Winchester, its work was particularly focussed on older people through the centuries. During the upheavals of the Reformation in the sixteenth century the role of the hospital declined, but fresh endowment resulted in the building of almshouses which meant housing became the Charity's new focus. In the twentieth century the Charity added to its historic almshouses with the building of new sheltered housing.

When I joined the Charity in 1987 I was tasked with developing residential and nursing care which resulted in the Charity building two nursing homes, one for the physically frail and another purpose-built for residents with dementia. When I retired twenty six years later in 2013 it was looking after nearly one hundred and fifty residents in a very unique form of continuing care community.[1] Although the Americans coined the term continuing care community in the twentieth century to describe a retirement community with a long-term contract that provides a residence, services, and nursing care in a continuum of care,[2] the aspiration of providing such a continuum of care has always been an objective of charities such as St. John's.

One of the things which made the Charity a special environment in which to work was the chance for me to work alongside the people we supported. It was in modern parlance a 'hands on' role in which despite the responsibilities of running a large organisation I was regularly in day to day contact with the residents, and I would not have had it any other way. Additionally I have been involved in pastoral support of many older people in the parishes in which I have served as a non-stipendiary Anglican priest. I have therefore been able to observe many older people meet both the challenges and the joys of growing old. They have taught me much, and as the years have gone by, I have realised that there are unique ways in which we can engage with what in this twenty first century is somewhat disparagingly referred to as 'getting old'. Having retired since I first began to write this, I have begun to gain my own lived experience of the third age.

Malcolm Johnson, one of the country's leading gerontologists whose work has been of great importance in encouraging a greater understanding of the ageing process, wrote recently: 'Everyday experience of living or working with older people, particularly those who have lost their independence, reveals that the ones who maintain a positive hold on life are far outnumbered by the depressed and the disappointed. For a subset of this unhappy group, the sequence of losses they have experienced leads to a state of anguish which steals from them many if not all of the pleasures of living.'[3] I fully respect that this reflects Professor Johnson's experience. As a counterbalance I can honestly record that whilst some residents at St. John's might have been ranked amongst the 'depressed and the disappointed', I do not think this would have applied to the majority during my time with the Charity. I think living in this community residents did find a generally more positive horizon despite the challenges, and I believe this was in part due to the Charity's aim of nurturing the whole person and therefore the inner spiritual life as well as the body.

The demographic changes which are touched upon in the Introduction pose huge challenges for our politicians and our health care providers. But this is not yet another book which seeks to grapple with those issues, although they do form a backdrop to aspects of what I want to explore. It is not a social analysis but a personal sharing of what I have observed of the ageing process and how to navigate it with special reference to our spirituality. I believe profoundly that ageing can be a positive experience and that we can see God at work in this, so whatever the challenges there is a real expectation of our experiencing a divine encounter in 'being old'.

I want to share this unapologetically from my own Christian perspective for the benefit of older Christians pursuing this journey right now, whilst at the same time affirming my belief that those who age successfully are those who have an honest awareness of their own spirituality however that is framed. In essence then this short book is a personal theological reflection borne out of my own story and experience rather than an academic study, of which there have been an increasing number of helpful publications in recent years. I hesitated therefore over the use of endnotes, but decided to use these as a guide to my sources and to point up opportunities for further reading. Hopefully those readers who prefer to read without the interruption of delving further will be able to do so. There is a bibliography which offers those interested a selective list of books that touch on the themes explored, but this does not include every source cited in the endnotes. Biblical quotations are taken from the New Revised Standard Version.

I have deliberately quoted from a wide range of writers, as my own reading and reflection has taught me that insight can be drawn from many quarters. This is a subject where we can all draw on the wisdom of so many different people. I am a great believer in the value of poetry to aid this process. It has rightly been said that 'poets are ...among the few in our society who explore hard subjects head on: ageing, pain, loneliness, the failing of the memory, and the inevitability of death.'[4] Whilst I hope the book celebrates the joys of ageing, these constant 'hard' issues are ones which we need to be able to address if we are to be spiritually whole in later life.

I am deeply indebted to the many residents of St. John's Winchester Charity whom it has been my privilege to know over the years, and also the many older parishioners I have known both in the Benefice of South Downs Gateway Churches Hampshire and in the Parish of St. Michael's Church Kirkby Malham Yorkshire during my ministries there, from all of whom I have learnt so much about how to age well. The ideas shared have been the subject of much personal reflection over the years, but it took some while to gather these together in a meaningful way. I am grateful to family and friends who have encouraged me to do so, and particularly those who have kept me up to the mark with regular enquiries as to my progress. If the latter have detected occasional moments of procrastination they may have been right. That said, I took comfort and recognised a kindred spirit when I read of the painter Renoir whose friends reproached him for doing everything but settle down to paint, to which he replied that a roaring fire requires the gathering of a great deal of wood![5]

Particular thanks are due to those whom I have talked with during the writing of this book, too many to record but everyone whom I have discussed thoughts and ideas with, and all those who have shared their experiences at workshops and retreats which I have led. Many participants on these occasions have asked me to share some of the material I have used, and this book is in part a response to their requests. The warden and staff of Parcevall Hall, the retreat house of the Diocese of Leeds, provided a refuge at a key stage in my writing and looked after me wonderfully well. I do want specifically to thank Ralph Court, Jan Michael, Alice Sachrajda, Angie Watts and Jonah Watts who read early drafts and shared comments with me. My daughter Alice gave me the sort of constructive criticism which only a daughter can give a father! The finished book is undoubtedly better for their input, but any remaining defects are wholly mine. I am immensely appreciative of the fact that Bishop Nick Baines found time in his busy work schedule to read my manuscript and contribute his generous foreword. Finally, special thanks are due to my children Kate, Alice and James for their constant encouragement and to my wife Diana for bearing with me so patiently and supportively during this lengthy process and indeed with the challenges of being married to a priest.

Michael Jackson
Feast of St. Barnabas 2020

INTRODUCTION

Being Old

In the late 1970s there was a boom in the building of sheltered housing. Some were planning a move into this form of housing when they retired or relatively soon after. When I first joined St. John's we had a lot of applications for accommodation from those in their seventies. Over the years since, the point at which people seek the support of sheltered housing has been rising inexorably. Many people are well into their eighties now, and St. John's had a fair number of applicants in their nineties. This is a product of the increased longevity in our society. One of the most notable statistics about age, of which we are all now so well aware, is that many people are living longer.

According to Age UK over the past decade we have seen a slow but steady increase in life expectancy. Today, on average, a woman aged sixty-five in England can expect to live another twenty-one years, while a man can expect another eighteen and a half. That is only the average, and life expectancy continues to increase. This is particularly marked when we consider that the number of centenarians increased by 73% between 2002 and 2012 to 13,350. Even more startling is the fact that a baby girl born in 2011 has a one in three chance of living to be a hundred and a baby boy has a one in four chance.[1]

By any reckoning we have a reasonable prospect of having a longer period of being older than past generations. What we can sometimes forget is that the prospect of old age as we know it today is very new. I was brought up short when I read the fact that half of the people who had ever lived beyond 65 were alive at the end of the twentieth century.[2] Looking forward to many years of old age is then a relatively new phenomenon, and we should not be dismayed if we are still exploring quite what this might mean for us spiritually as much as physically. Looked at positively this gives us the chance to be pioneers, charting new ways to be old.

When do we become old? A few years ago I tried an interesting exercise with a church Lent group which was exploring ageing by asking its members when middle age began and ended. Not surprisingly the older the participant in the exercise the later they left the end of middle age. I sensed a strong element of wishful thinking! Repetition of the exercise during retreats which I have led on the same subject has produced similar results. My grandchildren look forward to their next birthday. There is for them a sense of triumph in getting older. Perhaps one might argue with some truth that middle age begins when we lose that innate sense of triumph at the march of time or, as has been put a little more prosaically, when ageing becomes noticeable.

Not that long ago there was a general perception that middle age ended and old age set in with the advent of our state retirement pension, and yet now increased longevity has meant we often remain active well into retirement which blurs things and makes categorisation harder. Suffice it to say that although we all grow older by the day, 'being older' is a period in our lives most associated with the post retirement years. Perhaps the Beatles in their song *When I'm sixty four* were not far off the mark in setting that as the beginning of a period of being older. The length of that period is though much longer now than when they wrote of it in the 1960s, and the Lennon and McCartney lyrics would probably add on a decade or so if penned today.

The Beatles song had a wistful air of anxiety about the impact of being older on relationships. Today's great fear is the physical and mental consequences of ageing, and we do not always seem able to embrace Woody Allen's quip that ageing looks quite good when you consider the alternative! In a recent newspaper article actor Miriam Margolyes put it baldly when she observed: 'Nobody tells you that old age is going to be shitty. It's a kind of conspiracy.'[3] I am not so sure that I agree. On the contrary much of what we read in the press is depressingly negative. There are many articles one reads today which highlight how difficult it is to be old. These are often typified by lurid newspaper headlines, and I share just two examples which I have seen, 'The Middle Aged Dilemma: What to do with Mother?' and 'Alzheimer's: Slow Death in Dickensian Squalor'. Conspiracy, if there is one, sometimes seems more about painting as dark a picture as possible.

As a society we need to recover a greater sense of balance in how we describe ageing. The Bible gives us a good starting point. There is great respect in the Bible for the concept of age, and in the Old Testament this is emphasised in some staggering claims of longevity which reach the ultimate pinnacle with Methuselah, Noah's grandfather, who is recorded as reaching nine hundred and sixty-nine years![4] Mindful of that, it is perhaps not surprising that on being introduced to Pharaoh and asked his age, Jacob comments that his one hundred and thirty years have been *'few* and hard' (my italics).[5] The obvious hyperbole in such claims should not obscure the sense of reverence implied biblically in living to be old. A critical factor in these accounts is that really old age was extraordinary and praised accordingly.

I would love to see us escape from the modern perception that to be described as old is in some way a criticism or even pejorative. I know that I have my work cut out. The problem is that we go through a long period in later life when we think others old but not ourselves. Then when physical infirmity becomes an issue I have heard many mutter grimly to anyone who will listen 'don't get old'. My GP son tells me that he hears this remark several times a week. This is echoed in the complaint of the elderly Reverend Robert Broughton in Marilynne Robinson's novel *Gilead* that 'Jesus never had to be old'![6]

It may be that it is easier to move on to the more neutral ground of being prepared to acknowledge that we are getting older, if not old. I hope that having read this book readers will reclaim a sense of the value of being old, and the ability to join with the psalmist's lack of regret at this in proclaiming that 'I have been young, and now am old, yet I have not seen the righteous forsaken....'.[7] After many years as an epidemiologist working with an order of predominantly elderly nuns in the United States, David Snowdon rejects the wish expressed in The Who's song *My Generation* that they hoped to die before they got old, and argues that the grace and fulfilment of those he had been studying made him firmly hope to be old before he died.[8] It is my wish that this book may encourage such a hope in readers.

There are nevertheless differing degrees of being older. Sociologists have made a distinction between 'young old age' and 'old old age' which has been reflected in the division of later life into a third age of relative activity followed by a fourth age of increased dependency; these two are deemed to follow on from the first age of youth and second age of maturity. This division into phases of life is nothing new and was powerfully expressed by Shakespeare in a much quoted speech from *As You Like It*. Jacques comments that humans move from the first age of 'the infant, mewling and puking in the nurse's arms' through four more ages until:

> ....The sixth age shifts
> Into the lean and slipper'd pantaloon,
> With spectacles on nose and pouch on side,
> His youthful hose, well saved, a world too wide
> For his shrunk shank; and his big manly voice,
> Turning again toward childish treble, pipes
> And whistles in his sound. Last scene of all,
> That ends this strange eventful history,
> Is second childishness and mere oblivion,
> Sans teeth, sans eyes, sans taste, sans everything.[9]

One aim of this book will be to argue that contrary to Shakespeare's summary of a widely held view, we are never 'sans everything'. Hopefully though, we can like Jacques smile as we seek to demarcate how we see the progression of old age. Some years ago I visited the United States as a Winston Churchill Travelling Fellow to look at some of their continuing care communities for older people, referred to in the Preface and many of which are run by churches. I well remember one community administrator saying to me that he divided his residents up into the go-go's, slow-go's and no-go's!

Our lives are all different and we will bring to old age different experiences, good and bad, of fulfilment and of loss. A group of women in a Melbourne writing workshop are quoted in one study of ageing as saying that 'we should not glorify ageing or simply reverse the binary and equate old with beautiful'.[10] And yet, in an unusually optimistic poem *Beautiful Old Age*, D.H. Lawrence disagrees:

It ought to be lovely to be old
To be full of the peace that comes of experience
And wrinkled ripe fulfilment.

The poem ends:

And a girl should say:
It must be wonderful to live and grow old.
Look at my mother, how rich and still she is! -

And a young man should think: By Jove My father has faced all
weathers, but it's been a life![11]

This book seeks to explore the way in which we can draw on the range
of our experiences, to find the qualities which embolden us to face all
weathers and join with Lawrence in declaring 'it's been a life'. To do so
we should begin by looking at ourselves from within and forget pure
chronology. There is much truth in the aphorism that your birthday
only tells you when you were born, not how old you are. Some carry
their years very lightly. Although tragically killed in an accident at
the age of fifty-three, the monk and writer Thomas Merton was
described by his abbot as someone who could have lived to a hundred
without growing old.[12] We could all name people of whom that might
be said. And yet there are those of whom the opposite applies, like
Jane Austen's Mr. Woodhouse whom she tells us was 'a much older
man in ways than in years'.[13]

Spirituality

The focus for this deeper understanding of growing older is how
we manage to nurture the spiritual in later life. One study of this
dimension summarises spirituality as 'the human capacity for
participation in and responsiveness to the essential dynamism of the
transcendent'.[14] For the Christian this begins with how we understand
our creation. The Hebrew concept of 'ruach' is at the heart of a
biblical understanding of the spirit as the breath of life which enlivens
human beings. Its origins, as a word meaning both breath and breeze,

is echoed in both the Greek 'pneuma' and Latin 'spiritus' from which we derive the word spirit. It begins though in the first creative act of God recorded so magnificently in the beginning verses of Genesis when 'a wind from God swept over the face of the waters'. As Gordon Mursell puts it: 'In these few majestic verses something of the essential nature of spirituality in the Judaeo-Christian tradition is revealed. It is the process by which God created, and continues to create, all that is.'[15] It will be a theme of this book that there is a creativity in God's spirit within us which never dims.

There is a dimension of our lives which we categorise then as spiritual and an essential ingredient of successful ageing is being aware of our spirituality. For the Christian this is centred on Christ. As Mursell goes on to summarise it: 'Spirituality becomes just that: all of life, lived in the light of our relationship with God in Christ. It is integrating, relational, Christ centred. And it is transforming: we live no longer for ourselves, but for Christ.'[16]

It is important nevertheless to acknowledge that for some spirituality may not have the certainty of a religious perspective, Christian or otherwise. Wider definitions of spirituality as a search for the numinous and the transcendent in life are vital if we are going to embrace the widest level of human experience. The growth in literature exploring this has been a notable product of writing on ageing over the last decade or so. It is also increasingly recognised as an important feature of health care.

It is not within the scope of this book to undertake an analysis of the increasing range of definitions of spirituality, but one conference of researchers in medicine and health agreed the following: 'Spirituality is the personal quest for understanding answers to ultimate questions about life, about meaning, and about relationship to the sacred or transcendent, which may (or may not) lead to or arise from the development of religious rituals and the formation of community.'[17]

It is no accident that we have in recent years seen huge interest grow amongst health care professionals as much as religious leaders into what constitutes the spiritual. This was endorsed in an editorial in the British Medical Journal which highlighted a nursing textbook's citation of the following: 'In every human being there seems to be a spiritual dimension, a quality that goes beyond religious affiliation, that strives for inspiration, reverence, awe, meaning, and purpose even in those who do not believe in God. The spiritual dimension tries to be in harmony with the universe, strives for answers about the infinite, and comes essentially into focus in times of emotional stress, physical illness, loss, bereavement, and death.'[18] As these are all challenges faced in later life, it is vital we explore how to nurture the spiritual. It may indeed be that this elusive term is referring to religious experience without religious language.[19] I have to say that I like the suggestion that spirituality is the poetry of the soul and religion the prose.[20]

There is an old story told of a student nurse asking her supervisor where she could find something on spirituality. The supervisor responded impatiently, 'Look it up in the nurses' dictionary. You'll find it somewhere between sexuality and swallowing!'[21] I suggest we do indeed need to embrace the spiritual as readily as the physical in exploring how to engage with the challenges of ageing. That means a readiness to see the transcendent as much as the practical. The poet John O'Donohue's writing has done much to share that dimension and to celebrate the joy and fullness of a spiritual dimension of life which can get lost if we get too bogged down in defining spirituality. He summarises this so well:

> A true spirituality should have warmth and passion. The cold heart
> can believe nothing. There is a poised wildness in God that no
> concept can ever reach. It is lovely to find a spirituality which echoes
> the dignity of divine urgency and limitlessness. A true spirituality
> opens up the small thought-frames and the cages where feeling
> is locked; we come in to the mystery and intimacy of the divine.
> Spirituality should have great heart, a great flow of feeling that is held
> in worthy form. It should be able to show us again and again that our
> questions, needs and quest, our true longing, is already the presence
> of the divine, as the Lord whispered to the Lady Julian: 'Behold, I am
> the ground of thy beseeching'.[22]

Those who embrace a religious dimension on life like myself need to be aware of the growing perception that you can be spiritual without being religious. On the other hand whilst acknowledging that to be the case, it is important to share how a 'faith based' spirituality can enrich lives. To that extent what follows in this book is my own distillation of a Christian perspective on growing older. It is my belief that spirituality is not something one studies, but something one lives with Christ as the template.

Nurturing the Spiritual

The increased longevity which I have described means that many older people will experience physical decline in the later stages of their lives. Concern about this prompts many people's anxieties about ageing. Society tends therefore to see issues about this stage of life very much from a medical perspective, or as one professor of religion suggests as an engineering problem to be solved or at least ameliorated.[23] It is my contention that for the Christian we can so develop our spiritual life modelled on Christ that we can find ways not so much of trying to reduce the physical challenges of ageing but learning to live positively and imaginatively whatever those challenges may be. I do not seek to belittle the huge contribution which scientific advance has brought, and will continue to bring, in issues such as mobility and pain control, but it is important for each one of us to explore the internal opportunities for successful ageing as much as the external.

At the heart of so many definitions of spirituality is the voyage of self-discovery which it takes a lifetime to complete. We acknowledge that difficult period of life when as a teenager we desperately search to understand our emerging identity, but mistakenly we can fall into the trap of assuming we have acquired self-knowledge by the time we reach adulthood. In fact this is a lifetime's task. It is only in later life that we can begin to have the perspective to have truly divined our own 'cantus firmus', that firm ground of which musicians speak and which was so beautifully highlighted and explored by Michael Mayne, former Dean of Westminster, as his life drew to its close; what he describes as 'the absolute rather than the relative, learning to hold firm to the heart of the matter and sit light to the rest'.[24] There is a growing area of study into the correlation between religious belief and well-being in later life. It is not the direct purpose of this book to investigate this, and there is ongoing debate in academic circles about the extent of the connection. My own experience working with older people makes me confident that there is such a connection and I have been pleased to share practical experience from St. John's in some studies of this.[25]

The Church has sadly often failed to embrace the need for older people to nurture their spiritual identity in later life. It is not unreasonable for people to join with Anthony Trollope's character the Reverend Septimus Harding in asking 'what can a man's religion be worth, if it does not support him against the natural melancholy of declining years?'[26] In doing so we need to recognise that just as young people need to grow in faith, so do older people. It is a great mistake to assume that by the time people have reached retirement they necessarily have a fixed faith.

Those who age successfully are in my experience those who acknowledge the need to meet the challenges of later life by continuing to explore their spiritual identity. This has been well described as 'making your soul'[27], particularly as one nears death. Nurture is vital, or what Margaret Guenther calls 'crafting our lives'[28], and as she rightly points out many older people may have 'God-questions' without necessarily having the 'God-talk'.[29] It is of fundamental importance that the Church engages with this aspect of ageing. Its track record has not always been good. Happily though, greater interest in ageing and spirituality is resulting in initiatives such as the rapidly growing Anna Chaplaincy for older people sponsored by The Bible Reading Fellowship and pioneered by the inspiring work of Debbie Thrower.[30]

Some people in later life articulate a bleak sense of what is the point? Actually successful ageing is about tackling that question positively and engaging with the meaning of one's life. James Woodward whose wide ranging writings have greatly enhanced current appreciation of issues surrounding ageing and spirituality articulates some key questions as follows: 'Who have I been? Who am I now? Who will I be? What will become of me?'[31] One of the most important aspects of ministering to the needs of older people is in helping them to articulate all these questions for themselves. The answers I believe will lie in guiding them to a better understanding of the unique understanding that they have, as W. B. Yeats puts it, 'of what is past, or passing, or to come'[32] and it is those perspectives which provide the structure for this book.

PART 1

MAKING SENSE OF THE PAST

For you, O Lord, are my hope,
my trust, O Lord, from my youth.
Upon you I have leaned from my birth;
it was you who took me from my mother's womb.
My praise is continually of you.

[Psalm 71:5-6]

Chapter 1

IDENTITY

Grey hair is a crown of glory; it is gained in a righteous life.
[Proverbs 16:31]

Some people seem just to have arrived at old age, like Granny Seraphina in the Trinidad of *The White Woman on the Green Bicycle* where Monique Roffey shares this exchange:

> '....How old is Granny, anyway?'
> Venus went quiet and shook her head. 'Nobody know. She ent even know. Granny old.'[1]

For most of us though we count the years. One of the rites of passage which we all share is to navigate those birthdays which have a nought at the end; birthdays which more than anything else remind us of the march of time. Thirty may herald that our youth is now behind us and forty that middle age cannot be escaped, but with fifty the inevitability of ageing is a living reality, confirmed at sixty with retirement possibly on the horizon and at seventy with perhaps some signs of the beginning of physical or mental decline. Putting aside the mock horror which we proclaim as these landmarks are reached, it is vitally important to acknowledge the personal gains we acquire, which the biblical book of Proverbs collectively refers to as that 'crown of glory'.

One of the important spiritual aspects of ageing is to begin to have a sharpened perspective on our past. It is our past history which has made us what we are in the present. 'I carry all these memories and experiences within me. We are built from a shaky edifice of memories.

I may choose to travel empty-handed, but I have a full stuffed backpack of life that comes with me wherever I may go.' So reflects Neil Ansell.[2] I like the image, but we all know how easy it is to stuff things into a backpack. Later life gives us the time to do a bit of repacking and ask ourselves what is important and needful as we try and order those memories that are in the backpack.

St. Augustine puts this rather grandly: 'I will pass then beyond this power of my nature, rising by degrees unto him who made me. And I come to the fields and spacious palaces of my memory, where are the treasures of innumerable images, brought into it from things of all sorts perceived by the senses.'[3] Reconnecting with our past through our memory is a vital part of learning to live with some of the challenges of ageing. Indeed Goethe suggested 'we must plunge into experience and then reflect on the meaning of it.'[4] Finding meaning in the past is not necessarily easy and takes time. It starts with a sense of what has shaped us, in particular all that has given us our identity. Learning to identify a sense of our own identity is essential to a mature self-awareness.

We sometimes smile at the older person's fondness for stories of the past, but the retelling of these narratives is a vital part of acknowledging our identity. In doing so we can get in touch with the fact that there is much to celebrate in the story of our life. In her semi-autobiographical novel *The Professor* Charlotte Brontë's William Crinsworth rejects the cynicism of a friend who fails to see the full potential of his life with these words: 'You've only seen the title-page of my happiness; you don't know the tale that follows; you cannot conceive the interest and sweet variety and thrilling excitement of the narrative.'[5] Crinsworth has the self-awareness to understand the potential of his life. For many of us though, we may not be fully aware of the narrative of our life until we get a little older. We can then become more appreciative of how past events have shaped us positively and negatively.

Embracing the past rather than avoiding it, or burying its difficulties, is vital. Metropolitan Anthony of Sourozh, drawing on his wisdom as doctor, priest and finally a bishop in the Orthodox Church, argued that as long as we turn from our past we cannot resolve problems in the present or future.[6] It is never too late to be reconciled with those from whom we have become estranged. This is something which is explored in the later chapter on reconciliation. Not turning from our past means learning to be as comfortable in our skin as we can be and acknowledging the myriad of circumstances and people who have moulded us into the persons we are; for me, an example being in the dedication of this book.

The pace at which life moves means for many there is rarely a moment when we stop to reflect on how our identity has been forged. Many people of my age and generation have a host of albums and boxes of photos stored away, although no doubt in the future these will increasingly be on computer files. Using these as a prompt can be a way of reconnecting with the narrative of one's life and the people who have helped to forge our distinct identity.

This principle has been applied very successfully in a form of support for people with dementia in the creation of a 'Memory Box' which contains items that can stimulate the memory and connect people with their past. Pioneered by Faith in Elderly People, an inter-church group in Leeds, this concept has proved really helpful for those with memory impairment.[7] Careful selection of items to put in a small shoe box or similar container can become a valuable prompt leading people back to past experience and a sense of their identity. Those who were involved in this inventive initiative make a strong case that everyone should consider creating such a resource so it is available for possible use in the future, given that incapacity can affect us all suddenly and without time to plan such things. At the very least we would all do well to reflect with those closest to us about what we might put in our own Memory Box.

What we need to recognise is that we have a wealth of personal resources to draw upon. Viktor Frankl, the psychotherapist whose life's work on the importance of meaning was forged out of his experience as a prisoner in Nazi concentration camps, including Auschwitz, argued that we need to help people identify the spiritual resources which they may already possess, or want to explore further, to help them find meaning in their lives. Of older people Frankl wrote:

There is no reason to pity old people. Instead, young people should envy them. It is true that the old may have no opportunities, no possibilities in the future. But they have more than that. Instead of possibilities in the future, they have realities in the past- the potentialities they have actualised, the meanings they have fulfilled, the values they have realised - and nothing and nobody can ever remove these assets from the past.[8]

Whilst sharing the story of our lives is one way of connecting with the identity which we have forged over the years, we can also allow personal reflection and meditation a place in our lives so that we can better appreciate where God has been at work. This is a central tenet of our spiritual identity. Indeed a mature spirituality involves recognising that we have a unique story and being aware of how God's grace has worked in us. We live in a society where so much of our time is filled that we feel guilty if we stop the relentless physical and mental energies of the day. Spending time with God quietly and regularly will draw us closer to him, and can at the same time help us to see ourselves more clearly. Offering ourselves to God is a chance for him to gently throw light into the tangles and uncertainties. We can then begin to see how our narrative is being shaped and how God may wish us to shape it in the future. I am very conscious that there is something counter-cultural in this. Our society is all for doing, and yet learning to age well is about learning new more passive skills. Carole Bailey Stoneking puts it very succinctly:

> But modernity trains us that salvation comes not through listening to stories but by doing. Our "doing" covers over a religious and spiritual vision of aging that is biographical as well as biological; our "doing" covers over the vision that aging is an experience to be lived meaningfully and not only a problem of health and disease.[9]

Too often modern health care does see age just in terms of a 'problem of health and disease' which means the biographical is indeed sacrificed to the biological. Some years ago a leading elderly care physician Professor Peter Millard carried out an interesting experiment. Photographs of older people in hospital beds were observed by medical students firstly in stark hospital surroundings and secondly in the same situation but surrounded by personal belongings, ornaments and photographs. The students' responses to the second set of photographs were much more positive than the first, and the patients were perceived as more alert, stronger and more likely to improve. Helping the observers to connect with the life stories of these older people was the key to a different approach, and although not part of that research I suspect gave the patients a greater sense of their own personhood.[10]

When I have discussed this research at workshops or retreats on ageing everyone can see how logical it is that we identify people as individuals. Yet sadly there is still much that needs to be done in hospitals and nursing homes to uphold the identity and stories of those being cared for. It is many years now since a poem entitled *A Crabbit Old Woman* gained widespread circulation, before even the advent of the internet and the concept of information 'going viral'. The poem shares in the first person the life story of an elderly woman patient whose identity has remained a closed book to the nurses looking after her. The more recent revelation that it was written by a nurse anonymously does not undermine its force.[11] What has always moved readers is the author's challenge to look and see, to appreciate the old lady's story.

One of the fundamental keys to successful ageing is engaging with this biographical imperative in our lives, and I am sure that Carole Stoneking is right in identifying this as an essentially spiritual process. The Bible is brim full of life stories, both individual and collective. The Jewish people saw their history in terms of key people's stories from Genesis onwards through the patriarchs and the prophets, as well as in their communal narrative. The New Testament is also shaped around life stories and Jesus enhances that with his use of the parable as a teaching method.

Valuable as other life stories are and of other people to whom we are connected, we need in later life to reconnect very firmly with our own. It is then that we can see the pattern of our lives and those who have influenced us. Some years ago on retreat at St. Beuno's Jesuit

Spirituality Centre in North Wales I walked their outdoor labyrinth one morning, treating the exercise as an engagement with my life to date. Starting with my very earliest memories I paused at each bend to observe in retrospect the landmarks in my past and those for whom I could thank God as having influenced me and helped to form me. It was a profound experience, and for an hour or so I was totally absorbed in it. The thanksgiving to God began with my parents, siblings and wider family and moved through significant individuals such as teachers and mentors who had encouraged me or guided me at key moments of my life. It was a spiritual exercise which helped to throw my own identity into sharp relief.[12]

Such reflective exercises also allow us to see for ourselves the way in which God has been at work in our lives which the besetting busyness of life does not always allow us to do. The popular allegorical text *Footprints*, in which the writer in a dream sees the footprints of God in the sand alongside the writer's own, save for the moments when they become one set as God carries the writer, illustrates this powerfully. The moral that the writer has failed to realise the closeness of God is a failing of us all.[13]

When we are younger, or at any rate still have more than half our potential life ahead of us, we rightly have a particular focus on the future. As we get older and realise that we have fewer years ahead of us than in the past, we can look back in a reflective way and gain a better understanding of ourselves. It was the philosopher Søren Kierkegaard who famously suggested that life can best be understood backwards, but must be lived forwards. If we could chart the way forward on the basis of our past then life would of course be much easier. It does not work like that of course. As Coleridge puts it 'the light which experience gives is a lantern on the stern, which shines only on the waters behind us'.[14] However, it is worth bearing in mind that if we are always at the prow of the boat we will never gain the insights from that light at the stern, so it pays to make the time to stroll to the stern periodically and cast our eye on the waters behind. As we age we will in any event become more aware of the waters behind as the writer Penelope Lively perceptively reminds us. 'Not long ago, there was some kind of balance – a fore and aft, as it were. No longer; time has loped back, regressed, it no longer lies ahead, but behind.'[15]

It is not for nothing that I am beginning this exploration of faith and hope in later life by reflecting on how we understand our past, our story. This is at the heart of a mature spirituality. For it is how we begin to give our lives a sense of meaning and avoid emptiness and doubt. At the heart of the self-awareness of our own story is beginning to be at peace with the person we have become. 'One of the functions - one of the gifts - of old age is to become comfortable with the self we are, rather than to mourn what we are not.'[16] That is the view of the Benedictine nun Joan Chittister. Few of us when looking backwards cannot see moments when we could have done things differently, but it is crippling in later life to dwell on these moments so that we become embittered. There is no surer way to struggle with old age. Robert McCrum coins a good phrase when he counsels against the worm of regret:

> The lost experiences of former loves cannot be taken away, any more than life itself can be unlived. There's this existential truth: you and I might want our stories to be written differently, but it's our story, yours and mine, itself the sum of countless human transactions involving love and hate, fear and longing, pain and loss, anxiety, passion, risk and originality. Acknowledge this, perhaps, and you can begin to make peace with the worm of regret.[17]

Similarly, it is profoundly unhelpful to want just to bask in past success or achievement. We need to acknowledge those landmarks in the past which have made us what we are, but not to let them overshadow the present. William Wordsworth captures the essence of this very beautifully:

> Though nothing can bring back the hour
> Of splendour in the grass, of glory in the flower;
>   We will grieve not, rather find
> Strength in what remains behind.
> In the primal sympathy
> Which having been must ever be;
> In the soothing thoughts that spring

Out of human suffering;
In the faith that looks through death,
In years that bring the philosophic mind.[18]

It is important to acknowledge that our identity is forged by more than our own experiences. There are dangers in the individualism of modern society that we fail to fully appreciate our collective roots. We need to hold hard to the 'narrative that gives meaning to our lives'.[19] Culturally we do not give as much value to this as we should and as some other cultures do. In Christie Watson's award winning novel *Tiny Song Birds Far Away* set in Nigeria, it is grandmother, the oldest member of the family, who is the storyteller and who holds a divided family together with her stories about their shared identity.[20] This ability to share our stories becomes vitally important as we come to terms with the losses and disappointments of life as I shall explore in the next chapter. It is also increasingly important in our multi-cultural society to recognise different cultural narratives.[21]

Older people help to frame the story of the birth of Jesus as is so evident in Luke's gospel. It is notable that it is the elderly Zechariah and Elizabeth who are chosen to have an unexpected baby who will grow up to become John the Baptist and proclaim the imminence of God's saviour. They have endured the challenges of childlessness but God uses them as key figures in the gospel story because, in the spirit of the verse from Proverbs which begins this chapter, they have in reaching old age lived righteous lives.[22] Reading Luke's gospel account one senses that the two of them were very self-aware. Albeit surprised by the way God uses them, they rise to the challenge. They feel that age is against them, but end up being able to echo another proverb: 'The glory of youths is their strength, but the beauty of the aged is their grey hair.'[23] Luke also describes how two other righteous older people proclaim Jesus' identity as God's messiah after his birth, Simeon and the widow Anna.[24] It is these people who have the depth of experience to be able to see the significance of the birth of Jesus.

It is vital that the Church does more to harness the potential of its older members to share their stories and give positively to the next generation. Articulating how to nurture one's faith through life should not just be a preserve of ministers but a lived experience that is shared by older Christians.

Being aware of the lives we have led, reclaiming our identity and our personal story is the starting point for successful ageing. It may help us rise to the challenges of our final years. Connecting with, and sharing, our stories is part of growing into a settled old age. We need to give ourselves the space and quiet periodically to do so. We have the chance to look back on our lives, gain a renewed sense of the journey of life hitherto, and be ready then for the ongoing journey. As we do so we can begin to see the mysterious truth of those well-known lines of T. S. Eliot in East Coker:

> Old men ought to be explorers
> Here and there does not matter
> We must be still and still moving
> Into another intensity
> For a further union, a deeper communion
> Through the dark cold and the empty desolation,
> The wave cry, the wind cry, the vast waters
> Of the petrel and the porpoise. In my end is my beginning.[25]

Chapter 2

LOSS

Then Simeon blessed them and said to his mother Mary, 'This child is destined for the falling and the rising of many in Israel, and to be a sign that will be opposed so that the inner thoughts of many will be revealed - and a sword will pierce your own soul too.'
[Luke 2:34-35]

In the midst of the description in Luke's gospel of the elderly Simeon's blessing of the baby Jesus in the temple and his prophecy of what Jesus' life will reveal, there is this dark foreshadowing for Mary of the loss she will experience later following the savage crucifixion of her son. The loss of a child is indeed a pain that will pierce any soul. As we read this we can reflect how true it is that so often at the birth of a child we cannot know what will lie ahead in that life, but losses are experienced as an inevitable consequence of the lives we lead. There is a powerful painting in the Lady Chapel of St. Peter's Cathedral Adelaide by Penny Dowie entitled *The Foreshadowing of the Cross*. It shows a teenage Jesus carrying a plank of wood outside his father's carpentry shop. The sun falls on his body and the plank he carries to form a shadow in the distinct shape of a cross. Mary and Joseph look apprehensively on from the doorway. It is a painting which not only dramatically foretells the manner of the boy's death on the cross, but also his parents' foreboding about his future as well.

Old age offers us in contrast the prism of looking backwards at the losses of our past. One of the great challenges in later life is in coming to terms with accumulated loss, which is often accentuated in the last phase of our lives. Amongst the fears many people experience about growing old, fear of the losses which it may bring are often to the fore.

Anxiety over the uncertainties of what may happen to us are very real, but it is helpful to take stock over how loss has been navigated in our past lives. However difficult these may have been, they make us who we are. Brokenness is an inevitable part of what it is to be human, but I have always taken heart from the belief that we can become stronger in the broken places.

What we have to remember is that the onset of the infirmities of old age often come after the many accumulations of loss which a long life will have thrown up. And, they do seem to bank up as we get older. Take retirement for example. We are a society very much defined by what we do. 'What do you do?' is a ubiquitous ice breaker socially, but there comes a time for us all when we retire and lose that work-given identity. For some that can be a deep and painful loss.

As we live longer, many will go through more than one downsizing move. Of course it makes sense to move from a family home to a smaller one when children have left, and then possibly to a sheltered flat, and perhaps finally on to residential care. Each move, albeit based on sound reasons, can involve a significant loss of space-defined identity. In between the moves can come further loss with the shedding of possessions redolent with memories. We can lose a part of us when getting rid of items that have been familiar parts of our private space. The death of a pet, or the parting from one because of a move into care, can too be a heavy burden amidst so much change. Overall we can in old age face 'the thinning of the scenes of life by the loss of objects and interests'.[1] These accumulated losses during life have been called 'little deaths'; and are perhaps well characterised by what Wordsworth describes as:

> Some natural sorrow, loss, or pain,
> That has been, and may be again![2]

So the experience of bereavement, in the widest sense of the word as covering any loss looms large in later life. And it will of course also stalk many people's lives in the conventional sense of bereavement as describing the loss of a loved one; what the poet Dannie Abse describes evocatively as 'the woeful Now and the happier Then'.[3]

For some like Abse, whose wife Joan was killed in a car accident after fifty-four years of marriage, bereavement can presage a deeply isolating sense of loneliness. With characteristic clarity Wendy Cope delineates the sudden impact of widowhood in these terms:

> This is the future. It arrived so fast.
> When we were young it seemed so far away.
> Our years together vanished like a day
> At nightfall, sealed forever in the past.[4]

Another loss which can dominate in later life is the impact of disintegrating health which was powerfully conveyed in the words of Shakespeare from 'As You Like It' which I shared in the Introduction. We can smile at those words, but not perhaps if they echo what we are facing in the increasing loss of our own physical or mental health. We will then empathise with novelist Sebastian Barry's Annie Dunne who asks 'what is this growing old, when even the engine that holds our despair and hope in balance begins to fail us?'[5] There can be a growing sense of distance between our older self and a youthful time of greater vigour. This disparity creeps up upon us. Farmer Derriman in Thomas Hardy's *The Trumpet Major* echoes the thoughts of many: 'I am old, you know, and my poor remains are not what my original self was.'[6]

After years of advising and supporting others in this situation, during the first decade or so of this century I had to support my own parents through such losses. My father, who always needed to be involved in doing something practical, was deeply frustrated by the limitations of arthritis and a failing heart. Meanwhile my mother struggled with the onset of Alzheimer's disease, and of course the failing mind is a particularly distressing loss if, as she was at the outset, you are aware of it happening.

It was a painful journey for my family, punctuated by moments that particularly stick out in the mind. At one stage when they were still living in their own home, I was travelling to Suffolk regularly to visit and support them. Late one Sunday afternoon, as I prepared to get into the car and drive the three and a half hour journey home, my mother stood beside the car and suddenly burst into tears. 'I feel so frightened,' she sobbed. Unfortunately I had to get back home, and so after stopping for a while and doing my best to comfort her I had to leave her in the ongoing distress of Alzheimer's, briefly stopping outside their village to wipe away my own tears before driving on.

This is a distress always more acute for the sufferer in the early stages when they have knowledge of what is happening to them. After that my mother entered deeper into the darkness of the disease. The only saving grace was that as her memory diminished so did some of her fears. As she entered into a period of mental disintegration and the blankness of dying brain cells increased, it was a deeply distressing period of brokenness for her and all of those who loved her. Such experiences remind us of the fundamental nature of our minds and memory. Luis Bunuel, the film maker once wrote:

> You have to begin to lose your memory, if only in bits and pieces to realise that memory is what makes our lives. Life without memory is no life at all. Our memory is our coherence, our reason, our feeling, even our action. Without it, we are nothing.[7]

That is a bleak expression of hopelessness in the face of one of the greatest losses. When I first came across those words they echoed something of my pain at my mother's loss of memory. It was a dark desert experience for her and for our family. Small wonder that Samantha Harvey's novel about the experience of Alzheimer's disease was entitled *The Wilderness*[8]. And I found myself asking the same question as the poet Pádraig Daly in his poem *Alzheimer's*:

> How does the blank that keeps your features link
> With the glory that was you?[9]

It was indeed hard as it is for everyone faced with this experience, but I lived through the pain to a plateau where the experience touched a deep inner sense of what it is to be human. Let me put down a marker here to acknowledge that, and I shall explore this further in the later chapter entitled 'Passion'.

I need to pause at this point and acknowledge that I may seem to be painting a forbidding picture of old age. That is not where I want to leave the reader, but I wanted to set the scene by honestly attesting to the many challenges of loss which we face as we grow older; what one study rather despairingly describes as 'deep old age, a fourth age, with its projection of decline, dependency and decrepitude.'[10] The critical follow up question is how do we begin to cope with these challenges?

Years of pastoral ministry have taught me that individuals meet loss in so many different ways that it is difficult to generalise about coping strategies. Indeed, I think it can be demoralising for the bereaved to receive advice, albeit well intentioned and lived by another, but which does not resonate with their own experience. Loss is felt deep in our inner being. I can still remember vividly the words of a bereaved widower who was a resident at St. John's. 'I'm like one of those old trees you see in the country,' he mused, 'just alive, but largely hollow.' What a powerful simile that is for the pain of bereavement.

Whilst we can be cautious of coping theories, we can listen to those who share from their own experience. I have always valued Queen Elizabeth the Queen Mother's astute observation on bereavement, particularly as she had over fifty years of widowhood after the death of King George VI: 'Grief doesn't get any easier: you just get better at it.'[11] In contrast to the unhelpful suggestion which one can still hear sometimes proffered to the recently bereaved that 'you will get over it', the Queen Mother acknowledged what bereavement does feel like, a permanently changed existence, but she offered the hope that we can learn to live with it. The loss of a loved one leaves a hole in one's being that is a testament to the love felt for them. As one eighty year old writes: 'Love opens double gates on suffering. The pain of losing good is the measure of its goodness.'[12]

A moving reflection on bereavement is recorded in Helen MacDonald's best-selling book *H is for Hawk*. Not many will embark on the training of a goshawk as a way to surmount the loss of a much loved father as she did, but what makes this a life enhancing book is the light it throws on how we negotiate loss, going down routes that are deeply individual and painful, but right for us, and which lead to a calmer more measured appraisal of the loss we have suffered.

14

There is a time in life when you expect the world to be always full of new things. And then comes a day when you realise that it is not how it will be at all. You see that life will become a thing made of holes. Absences. Losses. Things that were there and are no longer. And you realise, too, that you have to grow around and between the gaps, though you can put your hand out to where things were and feel that tense, shining dullness of the space where the memories are.[13]

Reaching into our past to a place where we can put our hand out and feel our memories is where healing begins. In an effort to console, sometimes well-meaning people suggest to the bereaved that they will recover an illusory wholeness. This is both unhelpful and can be damaging. The vital thing to remember about bereavement is that although the hole of loss remains, we can heal around it. To lose someone whom we have loved means that our life can never be the same, but we can renew it. Dannie Abse shared the rawness of this in the journal he kept after his wife's death and also in a subsequent collection of poems.

...and she is both manifest and concealed –
manifest because I see her everywhere,
concealed because she is nowhere to be found.[14]

Although his journal *The Presence* finishes whilst he is still wrestling with the challenge of bereavement, there is a sense there of his re-engagement with memories on which a future is to be built, and it is the small things which loom large in his memory as they do for so many bereaved people.

Last night, lying in bed,
I remembered how, pensioners both,
before sleep, winter come,
your warm foot suddenly
would console my cold one.[15]

There can be a piercing intensity to grief that makes it one of the loneliest of human emotions. Sometimes we need to craft time for ourselves in which to heal. Robert Louis Stevenson wrote his classic *Travels with a Donkey* as he sought solace in France after a failed love affair. Christopher Rush, wrestling with profound depression after the death of his wife, followed Stevenson's footsteps with his own donkey and movingly describes a journey from grief to the beginnings of recovery. At the Monastery of Notre Dame des Neiges he finally finds the ability to reconnect with other people after the pain of only being able to confront his grief alone.[16]

One of the most important catalysts for his healing is the ability to talk to others. We saw in the last chapter the value in our lives of remaining connected to our stories. This means being able to connect with the lows as well as the highs, and importantly to share them. For some twelve years I was a volunteer with The Samaritans and learnt the profound value of helping callers to speak about their pain and sorrow. I discovered then some words of Shakespeare's which I have treasured ever since as expressing this so perfectly:

> Give sorrow words; the grief that does not speak
> Whispers the o'er fraught heart and bids it break.[17]

Finding the safe space to share our sorrows is vital to healing and spiritual well-being. In many years working with older people whose experiences have embraced a range of losses, I have always had a deep belief in the constantly creative force of God's love working in us to the end of our lives; for me a love manifested in the person of Jesus. Amidst the pain and suffering that Jesus encountered in first century Palestine we learn from the gospels of his overwhelming desire to come alongside people in their needs. This is compassion in the truest sense; compassion of course being a word whose origins mean literally to suffer alongside. It is no easy task. The hospice physician Sheila Cassidy highlighted this when she wrote that 'this is the meaning of compassion to enter into the suffering of another, to share in some small way in their pain, confusion and desolation'.[18] She elaborates elsewhere on the implications of this sharing of another's pain in these words:

16

It is this standing by helpless that is so difficult and yet so important, the simple being there to share in the suffering of birth, of living and of death. It is when we have nothing left to give that we are forced to open our hearts to share in the grief of the other...It would be so much easier to go away and do something constructive which would make one feel warm inside, but it is in the silent sharing of pain that love is shown.[19]

One of the key turning points in coming to terms with loss is in the experiencing of such love. 'Let Love clasp Grief lest both be drown'd'; so wrote Tennyson.[20] It is at the heart of the Christian gospel to 'bear one another's burdens, and in that way you will fulfil the law of Christ'.[21] We gain as receiver as much as giver of such love without perhaps realising at the time that this is taking place. Jean-Pierre de Caussade, whom I will introduce more fully in Chapter 9, argued that 'with God the more we seem to lose, the more we gain'.[22] That is a mystery which we can only live. Christians must guard against talking of the desirability of suffering, but we can attest from the testimonies of so many the ways in which we grow from it.

This means that we must not allow our losses of themselves to define us, but instead, by sitting still with God we may find firstly acceptance and then strength. The Franciscan priest and writer Richard Rohr has written movingly of the way in which in the second half of life we have to fall into loss before we can rise beyond it, so giving the title to his book *Falling Upward*.[23] Part of his thesis is that we have to experience loss in life to come closer to God. As he suggests, 'the bottom line of the gospel is that most of us have to hit some kind of bottom before we ever start the real spiritual journey'.[24]

A favourite American novel of mine is John Steinbeck's *The Grapes of Wrath* where the displaced Joad family lose their small plot of land in Oklahoma during the great depression and journey to California in search of work. The whole family is struggling with the loss of home and loss of self-esteem. It is Ma Joad who holds them together, her indomitable strength somehow forged in the losses they have experienced.

Her hazel eyes seemed to have experienced all possible tragedy and to have surmounted pain and suffering like steps into a high calm and a superhuman understanding. She seemed to know, to accept, to welcome her position, the citadel of the family, the strong place that could not be taken.[25]

One of the worst facets of loss is that when we are fully in its thrall we struggle to see the bigger picture. The grief that follows a bereavement can be both a numbing experience and all consuming. Old age gives us the opportunity for a longer perspective on loss, however difficult it is to always perceive. Simeon's words which preface this chapter must have been all too accurate a prediction of the pain felt by Mary at the foot of the cross. Our Christian faith is rooted in the love Jesus shared with us even to suffering death on that cross. Living through the pain of loss is part of what it means to love, and we will return to this later in Chapter 10 for Jesus takes us into both the pain and the hope of his passion. It is this that will help us to find hope beyond loss and join in the words of a Chilean prayer:

I believe that behind the mist the sun waits.
I believe that beyond the dark night it is raining stars.
I believe that this lost ship will reach port.
I believe I will not be robbed of Hope.[26]

Chapter 3

RECONCILIATION

For if while we were enemies, we were reconciled to God through the death of his Son, much more surely, having been reconciled, will we be saved by his life.
[Romans 5:10]

'The past is a foreign country: they do things differently there.' That first line of L. P Hartley's novel *The Go-Between* is often cited because many can identify with its sentiments.[1] However foreign the past may seem, and Hartley's main character looks back on childhood from his sixties, a key theme of this chapter is to argue for the need to engage with our past as we grow older in such a way that we heal the past.

A similar idea of the past is found in Kazuo Ishiguro's *When we were Orphans* where we find this exchange:

> 'One of our Japanese poets, a court lady many years ago wrote of how sad this was. She wrote of how our childhood becomes like a foreign land once we have grown' 'Well, Colonel, it's hardly a foreign land to me. In many ways, it's where I've continued to live all my life. It's only now I've started to make my journey from it.'[2]

Both these novels are suggesting a distant past that we can struggle to perceive in later life. Yet being in harmony with our past is essential if we are to have a spiritually mature grasp on life. Although Ishiguro's character Christopher Banks is suggesting he has only begun to journey from childhood to adulthood, we need to be able to journey the other way, into our past, and reconnect with all that lies there. I have already touched on how this is a place which helps to forge our identity and is sometimes shaped by loss. It can also be a place of regret and pain which we need to confront if we seek to emerge into the uplands of greater peace.

The distinguished gerontologist Malcolm Johnson has developed the concept of 'biographical pain' for the overwhelming sense of pain in an older person's past life. This he outlines in this way: 'The presence of serious biographical pain is characterised by the surfacing of deeply buried fractures in the life biographies of individuals who always intended to "put things right", but have now run out of capability to bring about that resolution. They will no longer be able to apologise, seek or give forgiveness, deliver restitution, deliver a good to balance out a bad or evil act. The opportunity to redress wrongs has passed by and the individual is left with an overwhelming sense of guilt.'[3]

It is helpful to identify this undoubted potential for deep pain and guilt, but I suggest that we can seek to redress this. For me there is an imperative in Christianity to seek to find reconciliation with God as we follow in Christ's steps, as the words of St. Paul which preface this chapter highlight. This needs to find expression in reconciliation with each other. My pastoral ministry amongst older people has left me with a deep recognition of the fact that seeking reconciliation with our past is of profound importance, and even if we have missed the chance to be reconciled face to face, it is my belief that it is never too late. Failure to achieve reconciliation can make death a far more fearful prospect. This process begins with forgiveness.

The petition in the Lord's Prayer to 'forgive us our sins as we forgive those who sin against us' is one of the cardinal tenets of any Christian's prayer life, and yet, as many would acknowledge, it is extremely hard to put into effect. It has rightly been suggested that inability to forgive is a locked-in syndrome that imprisons those unable to forgive in the memory of the offence.[4] Repeated repetition of those timeless words can dull our minds to the 'quid pro quo' of that petition. We are asking God for forgiveness in the manner of our own ability to forgive which, if we are honest, can sometimes be hopelessly circumscribed. One of the most destructive impacts on our lives spiritually is an inability to forgive. This is all the more so in later life when the harbouring of resentment may have taken deep root in someone's life, as may a nagging need for forgiveness. The Archbishop of Canterbury Justin Welby has spoken movingly of this challenge. In 1983 the Welbys' first child, Johanna, was killed in a car crash in Paris aged seven months. He has shared how he has struggled with forgiveness. 'I thought we'd sort of forgiven and dealt with that, but I realised a few years ago that I hadn't. I'd just shelved it. It revealed to me the depths of how one can deceive oneself. The costly road to forgiveness, that pain and agony, is something we have to tread if we are to get to a point where we can find reconciliation.'[5]

The power of forgiveness in old age is shared profoundly in Eric Lomax's moving account in his book *The Railway Man* of his struggle to forgive his torturers during the Second World War.[6] Taken prisoner by the Japanese, he was put to work on the infamous Burma-Siam railway. He drew a map of the railway and its discovery resulted in his suffering vicious torture at the hands of his Japanese captors. For years after the war he suffered from the psychological scars of this and was afflicted by a deep hate for the Japanese until a process of recovery began through the support he received from The Medical Foundation for the Care of Victims of Torture, now known as Freedom from Torture.

Ironically, the Japanese interpreter Nagase Takashi who was present at Lomax's torture was as scarred by his need for forgiveness as Lomax was by his inability to forgive. After the war Takashi dedicated his life to helping the allies locate the graves of prisoners of war buried alongside the railway, but he never forgot the particular horror of Lomax's torture which had so deeply affected him. The book recounts how through a series of fortuitous coincidences Lomax learns of Takashi's existence and makes a trip to Thailand where they meet. Their meeting as two old men, recounted at the end of the book, one wrestling with whether he has the ability to forgive and the other anxious for long sought forgiveness, is one of the most moving testimonies I have read of the importance of reconciliation in later life. It speaks powerfully of the importance of forgiveness as part of the ownership of the past and the striving for spiritual wholeness.[7]

American author and journalist Mitch Albom wrote a bestseller based on his account of the time he spent with his former college professor Morrie Schwartz as the latter was dying. Of all the advice passed on by the older man to the younger, one of the most pressing was his urging of the need to seize the opportunity for forgiveness. 'Forgive yourself. Forgive others. Don't wait…Not everyone gets the time I'm getting. Not everyone is as lucky.'[8] There is good counsel in those words on the need to use our time to good effect, so we do not 'run out of road'. Talking of which, there is an excellent 'road movie' to be watched in the film *The Straight Story* which engages movingly with this theme.[9] Based on a true story it tells of Alvin Straight who in his seventies learns that his estranged brother Lyle has had a stroke and may not recover. Alvin resolves to visit Lyle to make peace. Alvin has though just lost his driving licence for medical reasons and has over three hundred miles of the American Midwest to travel in order to get to see Lyle. So he hits on the idea of driving there on his ride-on-lawnmower! It is a powerful cinematic representation of the themes in this chapter. As Alvin says:

> There's no one knows your life better than a brother that's near your age. He knows who you are and what you are better than anyone on earth. My brother and I said some unforgivable things the last time we met, but, I'm trying to put that behind me…and this trip is a hard swallow of my pride. I just hope I'm not too late…a brother's a brother.[10]

Despite such good counsel it is very easy to prevaricate over the difficult task of making peace with those against whom we nurse a sense of grievance. The risk of death intervening and leaving us with words unsaid or actions untaken is something we can be aware of but ignore until it is too late, a human frailty which Charles Dickens touches on in Oliver Twist:

> We need to be careful with those about us, when every death carries to some small circle of survivors, thoughts of so much omitted, and so little done – of so many things forgotten, and so many more which might have been repaired! There is no remorse so deep as that which

is unavailing; if we would be spared its tortures, let us remember this, in time.[11]

But what if death intervenes before we have repaired the omissions of which Dickens writes? Should this result in unresolved guilt? Engaging with such remorse can be an important part of pastoral ministry with older people as I have personally found. Bishop Kallistos Ware offers wise guidance and makes the following telling point in answer to a real fear:

> All too easily it can happen that we postpone seeking a reconciliation with someone whom we have alienated, and death intervenes before we have forgiven each other. In bitter remorse, we are tempted to say to ourselves: "Too late, too late the chance, the chance has gone forever; there is nothing more to be done." But we are all together mistaken, for it is not too late.[12]

He goes on to emphasise our ability to seek reconciliation in prayer. Metropolitan Anthony has written in similar vein about a man riven with the memory of having accidentally killed the girl he loved. Metropolitan Anthony counselled the man who was wracked by unresolved guilt to talk to his deceased lover beyond the grave, seek forgiveness and then offer those thoughts to God so bringing peace into his heart.[13]

It is also important to remember that forgiveness is a two way process. It is as powerful to be able to forgive as to be forgiven. Finding the ability to forgive in later life is as important as seeking forgiveness. I have certainly seen the pastoral importance of this process of reconciliation, such as when an elderly widow shared with me how deeply troubled she was by her failure to forgive her deceased husband for his unfaithfulness. On his deathbed he had asked her to forgive him for an affair and she had found herself unable to do so. During her subsequent bereavement she was overcome by deep remorse over her inability to grant his request. We spoke together about her wish to effect this despite his death, and in a simple service of reconciliation held in her front room, she managed the forgiveness which had eluded her during his lifetime. This embodied for me the truth that 'forgiveness is a word based on 'letting go' for the sake of moving on, away from bitterness and hatred to a new way of being', words written in the context of national reconciliation but with equal implication for the individual.[14]

Our perception of where forgiveness is needed may be confused by the unravelling of events deep in our past. Early in my ministry an elderly parishioner in her eighties asked me to visit her at home. After a cup of tea she thrust pages and pages of notes into my hands with the comment 'take this away and you'll see what a bad person I am'. Back home, when I sat down to read her notes I was transported back into her past as a child. She had been born illegitimate and her mother had subsequently married a man who had put her through years of physical abuse well into her teens. As I reached the end of this grim snapshot of a violent past with tears in my eyes I was struggling to work out why I was supposed to conclude she was a bad person. In subsequent discussion a small passage in this account was highlighted, namely her mother's death many years later and her unwillingness to attend the funeral because of what she felt to be her mother's passive participation in the abuse. Her need for forgiveness for failing her mother had trumped any sense of her entitlement to be asked for her forgiveness for all she had suffered.

After we had talked through the way in which she had perhaps overlooked the fact that there were others more needing of forgiveness than herself, once again this seemed to call for a 'front room' act of reconciliation. This simple moment of liturgy had a profound impact on her ability to move on with her life into her nineties with a greater sense of closure on a grim past. It left me with a deep thankfulness for the extent of God's ability to mediate love in such situations, and the added bonus of her valued friendship until she died.

In different ways both these encounters which I have shared show how hard we can sometimes be on ourselves. As much as seeking forgiveness from others and forgiving others we have to learn to bestow that gift on ourselves. I fear we sometimes fail to remember Jesus' injunction to love in its entirety. His second commandment after bidding us to love God is that we should love our neighbours as ourselves.[15] Loving yourself in the truest sense is a gospel imperative which means according yourself measured and heartfelt forgiveness as you look back on your past once you have truly sought this from God.

Sometimes the enormity of what we carry from the past seems potentially too great for resolution and this is buried deep down in the memory. This can mean we carry hurts with which we have never been reconciled, and so the past can become a foreign country that we certainly do not wish to enter. This was something I was able to observe in my own father.

He was concluding his training as a doctor at St. Bartholomew's Hospital in London as the Second World War was nearing its final months. When the British army liberated Bergen-Belsen concentration camp in April 1945 quick decisions had to be made about how to help the sick and starving inmates. An appeal for volunteers from amongst final year medical students in London hospitals was made and my father was amongst the ninety-six who responded. Flown into an area of continuing conflict each medical student was given a hut at the camp and asked to do what they could for the emaciated former prisoners.[16] Their daily task involved deciding who had a chance of living and who was beyond help. Small wonder that the burden of this experience at the age of twenty-three was to haunt my father all his life.

For years he suffered nightmares and I grew up with the knowledge that this was a subject which was never spoken about in our family. Then in his eighties a chance visit to an exhibition charting the persecution of the Jews in Belgium whilst visiting that country resulted in my father engaging with his memories in a dam burst of recollection. Having not long since read Eric Lomax's *The Railway Man*, I wrote to my father subsequently to see whether he might like to consider a visit to the site of Belsen as a way of possibly helping to exorcise some of the demons in his memory. He took time to think about it and then said he would like to go. As a result my brother and I drove him to the site of the former camp in Germany.

Although the camp buildings were razed to the ground by the British army, there are poignant memorials to the dead and an excellent museum. After we arrived we were introduced to the museum curator who was delighted to meet my father and insisted in turn on his meeting a group of Czech women who as former prisoners just happened to be visiting at the same time. Now elderly they were making a similar journey back into their pasts. My father's instinct was to decline a meeting as he did not want any fuss, but the curator insisted. As we met these other visitors, one of the women embraced my father and said to him 'I have always wanted to thank the British doctors who saved our lives'. In this simple act of human contact she somehow dissipated so many years of pain in my father, and in the remaining years of his life he was able to talk of Belsen. Past memory was not erased but he had achieved a marked reconciliation with it.

I hope that the woman my father spoke with returned to the Czech Republic with a greater sense of peace herself. Another concentration camp survivor Edith Eger struggled to come to terms with her past for much of her life, and tried to blank it out. 'In running away from the past – from my fear – I didn't find freedom. I made a cell of my dread and sealed the lock with silence.'[17] In her autobiography she charts how only in later life she managed to come to terms with the unspeakable pain which she had suffered. Like many people who have wrestled in this way, she had to learn that to forgive is not to forget as some people sometimes mistakenly imagine. For as another Jewish writer puts it, 'forgetting makes no demands on the heart, forgiving does'.[18] It took much of her life for Edith Eger to understand this, until as an older woman she could find peace and acknowledge that it was not about pretending past hurts did not happen. After wrestling with these issues she could finally say: 'To forgive is to grieve – for what happened, for what didn't happen – and to give up the need for a different past. To accept life as it was and as it is is.'[19]

Returning to the image with which I began this chapter, both my father and Edith Eger had to remember firstly that which they were desperately trying *not* to remember. It has rightly been said that 'there is no healing of the memory until the memory itself is exposed'.[20] The novelist Sebastian Barry has a lyrical way with words, and in *On Canaan's Side* he captures beautifully the effort involved but the fact that it can be truly worth it. 'To remember sometimes is a great sorrow, but when the remembering has been done, there comes afterwards a very curious peacefulness. Because you have planted your flag on the summit of the sorrow, you have climbed it.'[21]

Matthew Arnold once said that we have to forget some memories because we could not live with them.[22] In a sense that was what Eric Lomax and my father were doing for much of their lives. The danger to our spiritual health of doing this is that memories have a habit of surfacing, however much we have tried to force them from our consciousness. Remembering can be painful in old age, but we do need to be prepared to revisit our past. If we do so in the right frame of mind we can achieve a 're-membering' which is at the heart of real reconciliation.

Whether we have struggled with forgiveness or a pain that haunts us, there is at the heart of our later years a need to be reconciled. I well remember a resident in one of the nursing homes run by St. John's who was dying but determined to make peace with her estranged daughter. Against all medical expectations she held death at bay whilst staff made great efforts to find and contact her daughter. This eventually was successful and meant it was possible for mother and daughter to come together at last. Happily this allowed both to find peace in the reconciliation which they achieved before the resident's death.

One of the powerful moments in Jesus' passion comes as the repentant thief shares his true self to Jesus on the cross and receives the promise of forgiveness. Jesus also amidst the horror of crucifixion finds the ability to extend much wider forgiveness: 'Father, forgive them, for they do not know what they are doing.'[23] There is a great comfort as we observe that moment of reconciliation on the cross. It is a reminder of the truth which St. Paul shares in the words of the Letter to the Romans which appear at the beginning of this chapter that we all find reconciliation in the love Jesus shared with us.

A deeply significant act of reconciliation occurred during the Second World war when after the bombing of Coventry Cathedral, two pieces of charred wood from its wreckage were raised as a cross with the words 'Father forgive'. By omitting the third word 'them' there was an acknowledgement in this of a universal need for forgiveness. Coventry Cathedral then put this into practice with its pioneering work seeking reconciliation with Germany after the war.

That is the same spirit of openness that will free us up in later life.

As we survey our past there is likely to be at least one person with whom we might seek reconciliation for one or more hurts. It is all about finding the right impetus as poet Pádraig Daly does when he picks up his pen for his 'Final Letter to Elizabeth'. The poem concludes:

> I write across the oceans
> That separate us now
> Begging forgiveness.
> Putting my hand out
> Lest either of us,
> The time being near,
> Should go out alone.[24]

Ultimately forgiveness is mediated through God's love. As Mary C. Grey writes in her profound theological reflection on the lessons of the Rwandan genocide, 'but finally, there is a gratuitousness in forgiving that must lie in the generosity and graciousness of God'.[25] If we are unreconciled with our past in old age we are in a very real way incomplete and not welcoming in the generosity and graciousness of God. It is customary as I have suggested in this chapter to speak of the state of being reconciled with those from whom we have become distanced, or with past trauma in our lives, as bringing us peace. The Hebrew word for peace used in the Bible is shalom. This has the added sense of wholeness or completeness, and it is that which I believe we acquire when finding reconciliation with the past in our final years. It is an integral part of a successful spirituality of later life to seek shalom in this way.

Chapter 4

WISDOM

Teach us to count our days that we may gain a wise heart.
[Psalm 90:12]

There is a long tradition that old age can bring wisdom. This is reflected in a splendid exchange in Charles Dickens' *The Pickwick Papers* between Sam Weller and his father. Dickens records Mr. Weller senior, who invariably pronounces 'w' as 'v', speaking with 'the gravity of age' and telling his son 'you'll find that as you get vider, you'll get viser. Vidth and visdom, Sammy, always grows together.'[1] If only Mr. Weller was right and the spreading waistline of later life was a route to greater wisdom!

When my first grandson to whom I am known as Papa reached the inquisitive stage of early childhood he often put my daughter on the spot with questions to her that he had clearly mulled over for a while. On one occasion after an obvious moment of deep reflection he asked her the question 'does Papa know everything?' When told about this subsequently it was a strong boost to my self-esteem to think that I was regarded as the fount of all knowledge in this way! It probably needs to be added though that my daughter tried very hard to answer Benjamin honestly without making too deep a puncture in his image of me. In a masterful reply she ventured 'Well, he does know quite a lot'. As well as making me smile, this experience reminded me that the potential for older people to help shape the next generation is profound. 'To influence even one child is to have a say in the future' suggests Michael Farrell in a novel it took him a lifetime to write.[2]

Knowledge is something which we generally respect and with it those who hold it. But knowledge does not necessarily make us wise.

I have always relished a story which highlights the distinction told about the great advocate F. E. Smith, later Lord Birkenhead, who was interrupted in court by a judge with this observation: 'Mr. Smith, I have been listening to you for an hour and a half; and I must say that I am none the wiser.' Smith's instant reply was 'That may well be the case, m'lud, but you are certainly better informed.'

Wisdom involves the right use or exercise of knowledge as opposed to its acquisition. It denotes a sharpness of intellect and also as the dictionary highlights, the exercise of sound judgement both in avoiding evil and attempting good. It is this latter element which makes it a quality highly prized in the Bible. There is a strong connection made between age and the acquisition of wisdom as the words of Psalm 90 which preface this chapter make clear. Indeed the Apocryphal books of the Old Testament highlight the quest for this gift in *The Wisdom of Solomon* and *Ecclesiasticus or the Wisdom of Jesus Son of Sirach*. That respect for wisdom is a tenet of Judaism from which Christianity has greatly benefitted. As Rabbi ben Zoma, a third century sage, wrote: 'Who is wise? One who knows more than anyone else? No. One who learns from everyone.'[3]

Most older people whom one might consider wise would probably acknowledge the truth of that aphorism in their own lives. It is vital then that we dissociate the mere acquisition of knowledge from any helpful way of defining wisdom. Knowing more than those about you is not a sign that you are wiser than them, perhaps well illustrated by Owl in A. A. Milne's *Winnie the Pooh*, deemed wise by the other animals in the Hundred Acre Wood purely on the basis of a smattering of greater knowledge. True wisdom has an innate quality about it which results from a distillation of life's experiences. There is an inner strength revealed in wisdom which is well highlighted by James Woodward:

> Wisdom is not what you know about; it is what you know, deep inside you, the essence of your inner life. Wisdom is the art of holding together the old and the new, of balancing the known with the unknown, the pain and the joy; it is a way of linking the whole of your life together in a needful integrity.[4]

Those words make so clear why wisdom is associated with age. It is in living our lives with all their challenges, inconsistencies and yet triumphs that we gain a sense of perspective on our lives. Wisdom is a lived quality. At its heart there is a strong sense of self-awareness. This is evident in the wise being people who are comfortable with their own identity and therefore self-aware. Those whom I would consider to have aged particularly well have all displayed this gift.

Some people have a natural ability to assimilate the lessons which life throws up, whilst others may have to work at this more consciously. Obsessing over what we have not done or achieved is a guaranteed way of making ageing more problematic. Indeed the negative side of doing so can become a real problem in facing up to death as we shall touch upon later in Chapter 11. Recognition of past failure or things we might have done differently can be used constructively rather than negatively.

Achieving that elusive lived quality of wisdom requires us to be truly in touch with our own life story. Story becomes so very important as we get older. We want to set our life in context. We can sometimes be too quickly dismissive of older people who retell the same stories. Children ask for the same story night after night so why not allow older people attachment to stories which they value. As I write this I have just said goodbye to a granddaughter who had been visiting from Australia and requested Beatrix Potter's *The Tale of Mr. Jeremy Fisher* virtually every night before bed. In the same way that children gain structure and familiarity to their early years in relating to familiar stories, we have an innate need to relate to the story we are each living out. In later life we may want to repeat what we see as the key patterns in our lives. Connecting and sharing our stories is part of growing into a settled old age. Culturally we have sometimes lost this willingness to relate to the way in which older people's stories contain truths for a wider family and community, what Ann Morisy has called 'spiritual capital'.[5] That spiritual capital is born out of life's experiences.

One of the joys of being responsible for the running of two nursing homes was the way in which I observed the residents sharing their life skills with staff. Contrary to the stereotypical image of frail older people constantly on the receiving end of care given by the staff, I know that many members of staff drew on the wisdom of those for whom they cared. They effectively acquired surrogate grandparents. This was borne out of living alongside each other. Modern family life which often means geographic separation of older people from families sometimes fails to allow this opportunity for drawing on the gift of wisdom in older people. The young can look to the old in this way for guidance and support. I have observed the same sort of interaction between my ninety-four year old aunt and the young carers visiting her in her home, many of whom sought her advice and guidance on problems in their lives.

I believe also that churches could do much more to make this connection possible and celebrate the wisdom of old age. They could also do more to harness this resource. Philip Larkin wrote a poem which explores the draw of entering churches even though he describes ending up at a loss as to why. In the concluding verse he senses it being a place 'proper to grow wise in'.[6] It would be good if that was an objective of all churches. Margaret Guenther has a good point when she argues that 'we need spiritual grannies and grandpas who have the time and the wisdom to wait patiently in out-of-the-way places of the spirit and quietly bring new things to birth in others'.[7] Hopefully a renewed interest in the ministry of spiritual direction is a sign that we can encourage more of this.

Asked what they considered to be the supreme good in their country, I doubt whether many people in this country would suggest our older people as a group of Japanese people did when questioned by Professor K. von Durkheim as reported by Paul Tournier.[8] Some cultures seem to have retained a stronger sense of this respect for the value of the aged. A few years ago I was at a conference on ageing and spirituality. At a reception on the first evening I found myself talking to a Hindu from the Edinburgh Interfaith Association. He told me a story that young Hindus learn of a man who has to leave his home in a hurry. He is told he can take just one valuable item. He looks around at his prized possessions, his money, his pictures, and then his eyes alight on his bedridden father. He instantly stoops and picks up his father and leaves the house with him as his item of value. 'We tell that story to all our young people' said my Hindu friend.

This reminds us of the significance of Luke's gospel account of Jesus' presentation in the temple which I have already highlighted where there was a recognition that the old in the persons of Simeon and Anna had the discernment to appreciate the significance of the child. Their wisdom is called in aid as witness to the significance of the young Jesus. In a poem reflecting on this, Ann Lewin catches the wisdom of well lived lives that lies behind this revelation.

> A moment of recognition,
> And they spoke about
> Fulfilment, theirs and his.
> For once old people
> Had the best lines.
>
> Age does not have to mean
> Diminishment. There may well be
> Constraints, but there is also
> Space and time for patient
> Prayerful growth to
> Wisdom's fruitfulness.[9]

I have already mentioned the film *The Straight Story*. There is a telling exchange in the film when Alvin is on the road and meets a group of bikers. He is asked, 'Must be something good about gettin' old?' To this he replies, 'Well I can't imagine anything good about being blind and lame at the same time but, still at my age I've seen about all that life has to dish out. I know to separate the wheat from the chaff, and let the small stuff fall away.'[10] In a homespun way that may be at the heart of wisdom. Advancing years allow us the space to sift life's myriad experiences and evaluate what truly matters. As Anthony de Mello reminds us: 'Some people will never learn anything because they grasp too soon. Wisdom, after all, is not a station you arrive at, but a manner of traveling.'[11] In just such a way Alvin Straight's wisdom is revealed in his journeying and not in the gaining of his destination. Letting go of the niggly problems of the past and yet retaining the resilience and sense which they gifted us means engaging with our life story in a positive way. It is drawing out the meaning through the perspective of age.

Thinking back to what was explored about coming to terms with loss, part of the paradox I highlighted then is the ability to hone hard experience so that it becomes a pathway to wisdom. In a challenging work entitled *Becoming Human* Jean Vanier explores paths to freedom. His third path is the wisdom that comes from unexpected events. He cites as examples the death of a friend, sickness, an accident that creates a severe disability, or an apparent misfortune that breaks the pattern of our life and causes us to re-evaluate our lives, so making us find new values. This is not the stuff of which we might normally think the wise are made, but Vanier's work with those with profound learning disabilities as the founder of the remarkable L'Arche communities gives him a distinct perspective. Significantly he suggests that to realise this we need an accompanier, someone to walk with us.[12] This is why we need to utilise the wisdom of those who have forged this in their lives. This concept of mentoring by the older wiser members of our community is something I shall return to later.

This chapter started by reminding us that we should not confuse wisdom with knowledge. On the contrary I would endorse the suggestion that 'the process of unlearning... is a necessary part of the spiritual journey'.[13] That observation of Janet Morley's was made as a comment on the way in which poetry helps that process. It is true that poetry does help us to filter not just experience but emotions so we can see the world through fresh eyes. The wise have that poetic ability. This can require the flexibility to adjust the trajectory of our lives as Vanier argues.

This can be a difficult task, particularly when we are caught up in some of the pain and suffering which will be the product of a long life. It would be wrong to ascribe wisdom just to the automatic passing of years, but it can be painfully acquired. Many have found comfort in the face of adversity in the Old Testament book of Job. It can be valuable also to reflect on what this book says to us about wisdom. There is a powerful exchange when Job responds to his supposed comforters with a mock reference to their supposed wisdom. He then asks, 'Is wisdom with the aged, and understanding in length of days?'

His immediate answer to his own rhetorical question is 'With God are wisdom and strength; he has counsel and understanding.'[14]

This reminds us forcefully that it is in fact in our deepening relationship with God that we temper life's experiences into an understanding that draws from our past and sheds light on our future. That is a gift of later years which is the foundation of true wisdom. When acquired it is a gift to be carried lightly. 'Show by your good life that your works are done with gentleness borne of wisdom' records the Letter of James.[15] In my experience the truly wise are at heart people of humility because they are always aware that there is more to learn and experience. This is rooted in an awareness like Job of the unending presence of God which we continue to learn about and explore throughout our lives.

Happily not all of us will be faced with afflictions such as Job's as a means to greater awareness of God's role in our lives. That said, we can learn from his willingness to wrestle with the eternal truths about God. There is no simple path to this process, but one thing we can do is to reflect on God's presence within our life stories. That means making time and space to do so. As Father George Congreve observes: 'By growing older we do not necessarily grow wiser or better. That happy change comes only as the soul grows in the knowledge and love of God; and prayer is the school in which it learns that knowledge of God which is love.'[16]

We are then left with some key truths about the elusive concept of wisdom. Neither the pursuit nor acquisition of knowledge guides us to it, nor does the accumulation of years offer us any guarantee of becoming wiser. There is though one guarantee of old age and that is that we will have our own personal life history, as unique as our own DNA identity. Old age affords us the chance to reflect on that, not in a judgemental nor regretful way, but in a realistic and appreciative way that sees the value and the gains. In his masterly and much praised exploration on what it means to be old, *The View in Winter*, Ronald Blythe quotes a poem of K. W. Gransden:

What is the secret of your long innings, sir?
Have you any tips to pass on to us?

-Try and grow used to the place of every star
And forget your own dark house.[17]

It is indeed true that the wise are those who have learnt to see the bigger picture in a 'long innings' and value it in their lives. For those of us who are Christians, that bigger picture is framed by the incarnate God who loves us to the end. Like Job we find our bearings as we survey the past in him.

PART 2

EMBRACING THE PRESENT

My mouth is filled with your praise,
and with your glory all day long.
Do not cast me off in the time of old age;
do not forsake me when my strength is spent.

[Psalm 71:8-9]

Chapter 5

GROWTH

So we do not lose heart. Even though our outer nature is wasting away,
our inner nature is being renewed day by day.
[2 Corinthians 4:16]

I find these words of St. Paul's immensely encouraging. In later life, as we experience the deterioration of health and our faculties are not what they once were, we could be excused for feeling life is just about decline, or 'prolonged dwindling' as one study of the fourth age posits.[1] Yet at the heart of living well as we age is a realisation that spiritually we can remain as active as ever, renewed daily by God's grace. Being aware of this can give us the understanding that we can continue to grow. I am grateful to James Woodward for highlighting some words of George Bernard Shaw's which summarise this very effectively. Shaw wrote in the Postscript to his play 'Back to Methuselah': 'Physically I am failing...yet my mind still feels capable of growth, for my curiosity is greater than ever. My soul goes marching on.'[2]

Although Shaw's concept is right, many of us might feel that to talk of our soul marching on implies an ease in this process which does not always seem present to us. It has echoes of Louis Armstrong's *When the Saints Go Marching In*! A contrasting and helpfully realistic approach is offered by Richard Rohr who having stated that we do not make or create our souls but grow them, suggests that 'we are the clumsy stewards of our souls'.[3] Amidst all the pressures of living it can take effort to look after ourselves, spiritually as well as physically, and we may indeed be clumsy stewards of doing so, but being aware of our capacity to grow is the first step.

There is something a little counter-cultural about embracing a sense of growth in later life. Perhaps this is partly due to the vocabulary of our youth when we talk of the process of moving from childhood through adolescence to adulthood as our time of 'growing up', so that we then become in every day parlance a 'grown up'. But it is important to remind ourselves that this does not mean we cease to grow. Put so baldly this may seem a truism, but there can be a worrying reluctance in society to accept that we can still be growing into our eighties and nineties. Some people even espouse a rebellious refusal to countenance this. Observing a car bumper sticker with the slogan 'I refuse to grow up' Sue Monk Kidd rightly comments that this is a deadly motto to follow in the spiritual life.[4] Being open to growth is a sign of a mature spirituality, but in fact truly growing up is one of life's great challenges. Timothy Radcliffe suggests 'growing up is emerging from the chrysalis of the self', and then adds 'this is the hardest thing'.[5] It is often only in later life that we find the ability to achieve this. I rather treasure his further suggestion that in St. Peter we all have a patron saint for late developers who take a long time to ripen into maturity![6]

Some of the challenges of increased longevity were touched upon in the Introduction, but the fact we may live for longer has also in a positive sense unlocked the capacity to achieve so much more in later life than our grandparents might have imagined. So much attention is devoted to some of the degenerative conditions which older people can experience that we can forget that the brain goes on producing new cells. The brains of older people may have become smaller physically, but this does not mean automatic reduction in capacity. The skills of reflection and analysis can deepen. Nurturing our minds can yield much. Ageing successfully is about harnessing this capacity for enlargement, and avoiding a self-induced mental atrophy which suggests we must be in decline.

The University of the Third Age movement (U3A) has harnessed this well. Its aim of learning for its own sake without qualification and with enjoyment at its heart allows personal growth without constraints. Learning a new skill in later life such as painting or carpentry may not involve becoming the greatest painter or carpenter, but it can be a sign of real personal growth. Growth in later life is less a physical fact and more a case of interior development. As Thomas Merton wrote in a letter to friends, 'our real journey in life is interior; it is a matter of growth, deepening, and of even greater surrender to the creative action of love and grace in our hearts'.[7] We can be attempting to satisfy our mind with new stimulation and knowledge, but growth has a distinct spiritual side. We can endeavour to steward our souls, however clumsily, but as Merton makes clear success in doing so is a response to God's love and grace. We find in fact this growing within us.

In his foreword to an anthology of Ann Lewin's poems Bishop Graham James shares these thoughts: 'One of my children, when just three years old, asked me, "Does God grow?" At the time I didn't think he wanted a detailed examination of one of the issues at the heart of process theology. But I've never forgotten the question. I was reminded of it time and time again when I read this new volume of Ann's poetry. I know that through her, my delight in the unexpected graces of our daring God has grown.'[8] This openness to God growing our awareness of his purposes for us is indeed a gift in later life which I believe we should treasure.

If this growth is at heart a spiritual process then it is vital that the Church engages with this. Sadly that has often not been the case. Too often there is a tendency to assume that we are fully formed in faith when we become older. On the contrary we need the same encouragement to grow spiritually in later life as we do as a child. The charity Christians on Ageing, formerly known as The Christian Council on Ageing, has tried to highlight the need for such an approach for many years. One of its key objectives has been 'to explore the Christian vocation and potential in later life and nurture the continuing development of faith and growth'.[9] Whilst the U3A movement has achieved a lot in encouraging older people to keep their minds active, the Church needs to embrace the need to help older people to nurture and grow their spiritual lives.

It is important to establish discussion or house groups in which older people can engage with long held questions and doubts about their faith. Recent material produced by the Methodist Church in collaboration with the Church of England in *Seasons of My Soul* has in my experience been a good way of stimulating discussion.[10] Giving permission for such a debate to be encountered is a vital part of pastoral ministry with older people. This means allowing older people to frame their questions rather than the Church articulating these for them. There is often an initial reluctance, but there can be a great feeling of liberation in exploring questions which may have been held back for fear that questions should no longer be a part of one's faith as one gets older.

It can be deeply inhibiting for older people to encounter an expectation that they have reached a perceived plateau in later life where their faith is regarded as static. To grow involves change and we need to embrace the ability to experiment and see the world through fresh eyes. One of the noticeable gifts older people often possess is the ability to travel lighter as they learn to shed some of the accumulated baggage of earlier years. Just as we have to learn to shed possessions which have become superfluous, we can shed those parts of our faith which have become formulaic and reinvigorate ourselves by relearning what is essential. If this is done constructively we can teach the younger generation as we do so.

I shall explore the gift of acceptance and waiting on life in Chapter 9. It is important to note at this point, however, that one thing that becomes increasingly evident in later life is that we can learn and grow despite seeming inactivity in a physical sense. 'To wait is part of the human condition. But instead of being a regrettable yet inevitable waste, it is a condition for growth, potentially holy and even Christlike.' So writes Margaret Guenther, a much respected spiritual director.[11]

Old age can be a time when we realise the nature of a relationship with God of which we may not have been fully aware but sensed deep within us. In his great spiritual autobiography St. Augustine looks deep into his own soul and finds after the failings of his youth he can sense this relationship and the fact that it is never too late. He makes himself open to this experience with the words: 'Late have I loved Thee, O Beauty so ancient and so new; late have I loved Thee! For behold Thou wert within me, and I outside.'[12] Augustine was not old by our standards when he wrote his *Confessions* in his early forties, but he clearly felt it was a way of himself as an older and wiser man learning from his youth and growing spiritually.

One of our greatest poets of the spiritual life George Herbert was similarly not an old man to our way of thinking, dying as he did just before his fortieth birthday, but he also wrote in a way that celebrated the growth that we can find in later life. His lovely phrase 'and now in age I bud again' is contained in *The Flower* the last three verses of which celebrate our ability to grow spiritually like the flower.

> But while I grow in a straight line,
> Still upwards bent, as if heav'n were mine own,
> Thy anger comes, and I decline:
> What frost to that? what pole is not the zone
>   Where all things burn,
>   When thou dost turn,
> And the least frown of thine is shown?
>
> And now in age I bud again,
> After so many deaths I live and write;
> I once more smell the dew and rain,
> And relish versing. Oh, my only light,
>   It cannot be
>   That I am he
> On whom thy tempests fell all night.
>
> These are thy wonders, Lord of love,
> To make us see we are but flowers that glide;
> Which when we once can find and prove,
> Thou hast a garden for us where to bide;
>   Who would be more,
>   Swelling through store,
> Forfeit their Paradise by their pride.[13]

Herbert's image of the flower budding despite the tempests of the night is one to treasure as we seek to emulate the renewal posed by St. Paul in the words which preface this chapter. The Scottish poet

Kathleen Jamie shares an image similar to Herbert's in her poem *The Wishing Tree*. One day walking in Argyll with her husband she came across a wishing tree, a tree where people would bash coins into its bark for a wish. She conjures a powerful presence out of this ageing tree holding the wishes of others:

> And though I'm poisoned,
> choking on the small change
>
> of human hope,
> daily beaten into me
>
> look: I am still alive –
> In fact, in bud.[14]

These horticultural images are helpful ones, emphasising as they do the capacity to continue to grow despite age. Every gardener knows of the need to cut away old growth to nurture the new. One of the tests of spiritual maturity is whether we have the capacity to do this. Jesus was fond of horticultural images, most powerfully in his comparing of himself to a vine and us as his branches.

> I am the true vine, and my Father is the vine grower. He removes
> every branch in me that bears no fruit. Every branch that bears fruit
> he prunes to make it bear more fruit. You have already been cleansed
> by the word that I have spoken to you. Abide in me as I abide in you.
> Just as the branch cannot bear fruit by itself unless it abides in the
> vine, neither can you unless you abide in me.[15]

Christians cherish this image of Jesus as the vine, but what does it mean for us in old age? A healthy faith involves feeding our minds with reading and prayer. Sometimes we have to jettison images of God which sustained us as children but are preventing a deepening of our relationship with him. This may be where a bit of pruning is required. The fact that vines often grow to a great age and produce some of their best fruit when they are older is an encouragement we should note. But as Jesus knew so well, vines need tending to be fruitful. At the heart of a healthy spirituality in later life needs to be a positive wish to encourage this process. Sustaining a sense of the potential for growth, of fruitfulness, is a sign of a spirit that like George Herbert's flower and Kathleen Jamie's tree is still alive, in bud, and therefore still growing.

Growth in later life can mean that we can be recognised even then for our fruit and our enjoyment of halcyon days as Walt Whitman celebrates:

> Not from successful love alone,
> Nor wealth, nor honor'd middle age, nor victories of politics
> or war;
> But as life wanes, and all the turbulent passions calm,
> As gorgeous, vapory, silent hues cover the evening sky,
> As softness, fulness, rest, suffuse the frame, like fresher,
> balmier air,
> As the days take on a mellower light, and the apple at last
> hangs really finish'd and indolent-ripe on the tree,
> Then for the teeming quietest, happiest days of all!
> The brooding and blissful halcyon days![16]

There is a simple message which we can draw from these reflections. We are all conversant with the concept of our growing older. Many people perceive this to be symptomatic of decline. In contrast, we need to remind ourselves of our inner nature being renewed each day as St. Paul reminds us. This God given dynamic of our soul will then teach us that growing older is a promise of growing *as* we get older.

Even more significantly this will allow us to embrace life until it is brought to an end by death. Seeing later life as decline will become a self-fulfilling prophecy. In contrast, seizing each moment for growth allows us to celebrate living as opportunity right to the end. This is beautifully explored by novelist and poet Helen Dunmore in her final collection of poems, *Inside the Wave*, posthumously awarded the Costa Prize. Even when faced with a terminal diagnosis she can see her life as a cut flower that is still flowering:

I know I am dying
But why not keep flowering
As long as I can
From my cut stem?[17]

Chapter 6

CONTENTMENT

Of course, there is great gain in godliness combined with contentment; for we brought nothing into the world, so that we can take nothing out of it; but if we have food and clothing, we will be content with these.
[1 Timothy 6:6]

I was going to entitle this chapter 'happiness'. I shied away from this in part because of a nervousness about a modern tendency to prize happiness so highly that we can make it an unattainable goal amidst the vicissitudes of daily living, notwithstanding the multitude of self-help manuals which can be purchased with this declared goal. The former Chief Rabbi has rightly pointed out that happiness is elusive and you do not find it by pursuing it.[1] Indeed the novelist Graham Greene suggested happiness goes when you speak of it.[2] There is though a joy to life which we know when we experience it and which is at the heart of a fulfilled life.

I decided to opt for 'contentment' as this chapter heading because it is an all-encompassing word which can include the highs of happiness and humour, but also the ability to enjoy life for what it is, not straining for the unachievable but happy in the moment. In its meaning of satisfaction of mind contentment may have a more neutral ring about it, but it is a word which denotes one of the key stabilising qualities of later life. 'Time hasn't aged us, it has contented us,' reflects Hiroko in Kamila Shamsie's epic novel *Burnt Shadows*.[3]

The words which preface this chapter from the First Letter of St. Paul to Timothy remind us to approach life with a sense of satisfaction for what we have. We hear the middle words of that quotation less often at funerals than used to be the case, but that association is a good reminder of the sound advice being proffered in this letter for

47

our inevitably finite lives. It is much easier to be happy as we age if we start from this premise. The challenges which I explored earlier will undoubtedly bring moments of unhappiness which can cause us to waiver if we have placed happiness on a pedestal.

Contentment is borne out of what we have and not what we would rather have. St Paul comments further in his letter to the Philippians:

> Not that I am referring to being in need; for I have learned to be content with whatever I have. I know what it is to have little, and I know what it is to have plenty. In any and all circumstances I have learned the secret of being well-fed and of going hungry, of having plenty and of being in need. I can do all things through him who strengthens me.[4]

Some older people slip almost imperceptibly into a form of permanent melancholy. This is typified by an overwhelming awareness of the difficulties they face so they are quite simply gloomy about all that they experience. At its worse such a state of mind extends beyond personal unhappiness into a cynicism about others. The fact that old age can produce real challenges to the human will has already been acknowledged. There should however be no assumption that sadness must dog us for ever. Melancholy has a tendency to cut people off from those about them. Conversely contentment will draw one to others, valuing their company and what they have to share. In doing so it brings a gift to others.

It is worrying that depression amongst older people continues to be a major mental health concern. For some there will be the need for psychiatric intervention, and I have witnessed some exceptional community based elderly care psychiatry. This book approaches later life from the dimension of our spiritual well-being, something which we can do much to nurture for ourselves, but anxiety can nevertheless impact on this. Worry is not a new phenomenon. It is intrinsic to human existence. Jesus addressed it directly with his trenchant comments in St. Matthew's Gospel where he urges listeners 'do not worry about your life'.[5] He urges us to put aside concern even about food and clothing. The punchline in his teaching is not that these things do not matter, nor that worry will not sometimes challenge us, but that life is about priorities where striving for the kingdom of God comes first and all else will follow.

Placing God's purposes at the heart of our lives gives us a compass bearing in the journey of life. This is of fundamental importance as we get older when, as has been described, difficulties can hem us in. There is no one way to achieve this, but heeding Jesus' words and seeking to build the kingdom of God will mean engaging with life in a spiritually enriching way as we shall explore in the next chapter. Contentment is then about holding hard to God as our compass whatever the circumstances we face.

I like to think that contentment breeds a readiness to see the funny side of life. This is a prescription for easing some of the difficulties of ageing as is recognised in the book of Proverbs in the Old Testament where we read that 'a cheerful heart is a good medicine, but a downcast spirit dries up the bones'.[6] As so often the writer of this proverb has compressed much wisdom into a short sentence. This connection is made by many, as for example by Anne Brontë who wrote that there is nothing like a cheerful mind for keeping the body in health.[7] Indeed the book of Ecclesiasticus suggests a connection with longevity when declaring 'a joyful heart is life itself, and rejoicing lengthens one's life span'.[8] The writer even continues by commending it for digestion as 'those who are cheerful and merry at table will benefit from their food'![9]

Humour is undoubtedly good for us. More to the point, by contrasting the medicinal properties of good cheer with a downcast spirit the author of Proverbs is highlighting that humour has a spiritual dimension and should not be idly dismissed just as a frivolous bonus in life. Time and time again during my time at St. John's I was struck by the way that humour is a gift that we can share with each other as we age. As such it becomes a spiritual gift to others.

I shall always remember with particular affection Dolly, a resident in one of the Charity's nursing homes who had suffered a severe stroke before she was admitted. She had lost the power of coherent speech but she could still smile and laugh. Her sense of fun lit up whichever room she was in; so much so that when she died there was a deep void in the home, felt by both residents and staff. This was a void left by a lady who had never shared a word with us but who had constantly shared her infectious smile and laughter.

Dolly taught me that the ability to laugh can override seemingly devastating challenges. Her story reminds us that this can always be found. John Betjeman captured the essence of this gift in his delightful little poem *The Last Laugh* where he shared these thoughts:

> I made hay whilst the sun shone.
> My work sold.
> Now, if the harvest is over
> And the world cold,
> Give me the bonus of laughter.[10]

Living with my mother's dementia was a time when the world had indeed become 'cold' for our family, and yet there were moments when shafts of laughter parted the overwhelming sadness of her mental decline. As a family we tried to laugh at some of the more bizarre moments during her illness, laughing with her whenever possible, such as when it gently had to be explained to her that she was about to offer her dog a can of lager rather than dog food! I can still treasure the moment when the reality of what she was attempting to do dawned on her and she led the ensuing laughter as we laughed with her rather than at her. It is important in later life to cherish life's absurdities, the idiosyncrasies, and the comical.

The late, and much lamented, Rabbi Lionel Blue's contributions to 'Thought for the Day' on Radio 4 often achieved just that and were much appreciated in consequence. In the earlier years of these broadcasts he used to refer quite often to the problems of caring for his elderly mother and he would bring into his radio slots things that arose on visiting her in her residential home. On one occasion he told the story of the rather pompous local dignitary visiting the Home. I think it may have been the local MP who decided to do some canvassing there. The visitor was a bit disconcerted when one old lady he stopped to speak to did not seem to recognise him. 'Don't you know who I am?' he asked. This produced the considered response:

'No dear, but don't worry about it. Go and ask Matron and she'll tell you.' I have shared that story with many groups of older people and it never fails to produce ready laughter. Another popular one which I have passed on is a comic aphorism on a fridge magnet which the nurses had stuck on the drugs safe in one of the nursing homes at St. John's. It simply read 'be nice to your children....they'll choose your nursing home'!

In Umberto Eco's *The Name of the Rose* there is a moment when a monk chides a visitor to his monastery for presuming to think that Christ ever laughed, calling in aid the great fourth century theologian John Chrysostom.[11] I think that says more about the buttoned up nature of the angry monk than the likely nature of Jesus. His humanity shines through the gospels. In the choice of parables as a teaching method I am confident that Jesus elicited many a smile and a laugh, such as when his audience reflected on the impossibility of a camel being threaded through the eye of a needle. So, I am sure it is important to see the potential for the divine in laughter. American author Sue Monk Kidd tells of her daughter questioning whether God laughs. 'Why do you ask?' she enquires, to be met with the reply 'Because I think I heard him today'![12] If we are spiritually whole we should be able to hear God joining in our laughter.

The well-known seven deadly sins were originally eight when penned by Evagrius in the fourth century. Pope Gregory the Great reduced them to seven and in the process we lost Evagrius' sin of sadness; there because it was deemed to indicate a lack of hope. In his corresponding list of virtues Evagrius had extolled 'hilaritas' or laughter. It is to me a cause for regret that possibly in consequence of this the Church somehow came to lose the celebration of laughter as an intrinsic virtue. Indeed St. Benedict's monastic Rule specifically forbade words that move to laughter.[13] There has been a long tradition of unease, at the very least, over laughter in churches, no doubt based around a fear that it might lead to levity over the serious business of faith. Happily the last few decades have seen a greater willingness to accept the place of laughter. I was encouraged to read of a Roman Catholic convent where women were only admitted to the novitiate if they ate well, slept well, and laughed easily.[14] The challenge remains though for there to be an avowed belief in the power of laughter as a key component of our spiritual lives, and acknowledgement that this is never more essential than as we age.

Laughter is but a reflection of the 'joyful heart' commended in Ecclesiasticus. There is something which marks out people who have developed this willingness to find joy in their lives. People like this do not just laugh easily, they find contentment in all about them. Those who are truly content have a spiritual gift of serenity to impart to others. Contemporaries of the playwright and essayist Joseph Addison observed that his serenity was capable of rising above the disappointments of his life, and for that considerable virtue he was widely loved.[15] One of the gifts of Jane Austen as a novelist was to bring alive the minor characters in her books. She offers us a wonderful portrait of the sort of life I am highlighting when she introduces us to Miss Bates:

> She had never boasted either beauty or cleverness. Her youth had passed without distinction, and her middle of life was devoted to the care of a failing mother, and the endeavour to make a small income go as far as possible. And yet she was a happy woman, and a woman whom no one named without good-will. It was her own universal good-will and contented temper which worked such wonders. She loved every body, was interested in every body's happiness, quick sighted to every body's merits; thought herself a most fortunate creature, and surrounded with blessings in such an excellent mother and so many good neighbours and friends, and a home that wanted for nothing. The simplicity and cheerfulness of her nature, her contented and grateful spirit, were a recommendation to every body and a mine of felicity to herself.[16]

It is not surprising that literature offers us a ready path into this exploration of what can be an elusive quality to describe. In his Booker prize winning novel *The Remains of the Day* Kazuo Ishiguro shares an elegiac portrait of the reflectiveness of later life as the central character Stevens makes some sense of his past and despite its disappointments realises there is still a chance of seeking a sense of contentment. He has a conversation with a stranger who urges:

You've got to enjoy yourself. The evening's the best part of the day. You've done your day's work. Now you can put your feet up and enjoy it. That's how I look at it. Ask anybody, they'll tell you. The evening's the best part of the day.'

As he thinks on this advice Stevens concludes:

> Perhaps, then, there is something to his advice that I should cease looking back so much, that I should adopt a more positive outlook and try to make the best of what remains of my day. After all, what can we ever gain in forever looking back and blaming ourselves if our lives have not turned out quite as we might have wished? .....What is the point in worrying oneself too much about what one could or could not have done to control the course one's life took? Surely it is enough that the likes of you and me at least *try* to make a small contribution count for something true and worthy. And if some of us are prepared to sacrifice much in life in order to pursue such aspirations, surely that is in itself, whatever the outcome, cause for pride and contentment.[17]

One of the things that Stevens comes to realise is that contentment is not just handed to us on a plate as we reach the latter part of our life. The emphasis on the word 'try' in that passage is rightly made by Ishiguro. Florida Scott-Maxwell to whom I have already referred would agree:

> The old can be tranquil but it is an achievement. If at the end we choose to represent tranquillity, as without us it might be missing, let it be clearly seen that tranquillity is not a grace waiting for us to take as our right, but something we have to win with effort. It may not be our doing. It may be what facing age does to us. Then here lies our victory.[18]

So, elusive as it may be, I want to suggest that contentment in later life is indeed a spiritual gift. It is often the better for being unsought but honed through the way we live and engage with those about us.

53

Mindful of the title of this book we will have achieved this if in our later years we are known for our love and can achieve the 'mild passive happiness of love-crowned age' as achieved by George Eliot's Silas Marner at the end of his life.[19] Those who have enjoyed this much loved novel will be aware that Marner's love-crowned age comes only after he has been wrongly accused of theft and withdrawn from society. It is in the love he gives to his adopted daughter Eppie that he achieves redemption. He finds serenity by transfiguring the pain of his earlier life. Contentment is the life affirming product of the love in his life.

Ultimately, at the heart of contentment is a recognition that we draw on God's love in all he shares with us, just as the psalmist celebrates: 'How precious is your steadfast love, O God! All people may take refuge in the shadow of your wings. They feast on the abundance of your house, and you give them drink from the river of your delights. For with you is the fountain of life; in your light we see light.'[20] This is a recognition which will allow us to pray with conviction in the words of a retired priest in India: 'O God, whose love has kept me vigorously and joyfully at work in days gone by, and now sends me joyful and contented into silence and inactivity, grant that I may find happiness in you in all my solitary and quiet hours. Amen.'[21]

Chapter 7

ENGAGEMENT

Therefore devote yourselves completely to the Lord our God,
walking in his statutes and keeping his commandments,
as at this day.
[1 Kings 8:61]

'Dear me! What shall you do? How shall you employ yourself when you grow old?' So an anxious Harriet Smith asks Jane Austen's Emma.[1] There is sometimes a worrying perception that ageing is inevitably a time of diminishment with an inability to engage with anything constructive. This can be fuelled by negative media coverage, and feed a sense of lowering expectation as we get older. It is important to resist this tendency, and assert the need to renew our efforts to live as fully as we can and relate positively with all about us. Solomon's injunction in the Old Testament book of 1 Kings which prefaces this chapter remains good whatever our age. God calls us to be engaged with living and to fulfil his wishes for us. It is of particular importance that we have a sense of purpose. Many modern studies of ageing confirm that retaining this is vital for fulfilment in later life.

I have already alluded to the way in which retirement can for some be a deep loss. Work can become so all-consuming that it is perceived as the only way to fully engage in society, but it can come at a price. In fact retirement can offer new opportunities which were not previously possible. This can start with time for families and grandchildren if we have them. It can also extend to new activities. There is a strong correlation here with the need to grow in later life. You could say that 'engagement', as I have called this chapter, is about the energy with which we apply ourselves as we grow. We are considering here qualities which help us to engage with all that goes on and thereby to age well. As Sister Joan Chittister writes: 'Aging well is the real goal of life. To allow ourselves to age without vitality, without energy, without purpose, without growth is simply to get old rather than to age well as we go.'[2]

Although retirement can be a worrying time for some, it opens up a range of potential activity which is wide ranging in its potential. Compared with previous generations there is so much opportunity to stay focussed on the world in which we live. The opportunity to give time voluntarily allows the retired to make a really positive impact on society. Many voluntary organisations need and welcome this with open arms. As a life-long reader I have recently joined my local library's Home Library Scheme which involves sourcing books for the housebound; a small investment of my time is allowing other book lovers less physically able than me to remain engaged in reading. Mentoring schemes where older people have a chance to share experience with the younger generation are also valuable for all involved, and a practical way of sharing time tested wisdom. Active engagement with life so that we continue to learn to fulfill our potential is a pre-requisite to achieving wisdom in the first place.

Fundamentally this ability to engage in new opportunities for voluntary activities is one of time. Throughout our working lives we are in thrall to the clock. The lack of time to do all that we would like to do can be a very real brake on our achieving all that we should like. This book began to germinate in my mind some years back, but it was not until retirement that I found the time to write it, albeit that it has taken longer to complete than I intended because of the lack of time constraints! Retirement unlocks a more measured use of time. We can stay engaged, but at our pace. And we should not be shy of the recreational side of the time at our disposal. The word recreation derives from the Latin 'recreare' which means literally 'to create anew'. There is an important spiritual dimension to giving time to such re-creation.

Being creative is a way of expanding our souls as much as our minds. An interesting study by Susan A. Eisenhandler has shown the positive advantages of gardening in an American retirement community in Connecticut where everyone has their own patch of garden. 'It is not, as many people suggest to me in talks and discussions that gardening is "therapeutic", as it well may be; it is instead that gardening is a part of living and being, an otherwise readily adopted activity that moves its adherents and practitioners beyond the profane and the ordinary for varied periods of time.' She goes on to say that: 'Gardening confers an inexpressible connection to human existence that other creative activities such as music, art, poetry, dance, and religious faith and spirituality offer to their participants. Such joy in living may indeed be partial and ineffable but it is the soul singing a full-hearted evensong.'[3] Recalling my earlier consideration of the notion of spirituality, I emphasised how this is rooted in an exploration of meaning in our lives. Eisenhandler is right to tease out how creativity fosters this and enhances the evensong of life.

A key message for us all is that age should not be a bar to creativity, or indeed activity, within the bounds of our frailties. The last years of the painter Henri Matisse are a good example of this. Confined to a wheelchair Matisse struggled to paint as he had done earlier in his life but discovered that he could still give rein to his creativity by 'painting with scissors' as he put it. He would cut shapes out with scissors and then arrange them using a long stick, so continuing to be engaged creatively until his death.[4]

A very special friend of mine used her active involvement in a local U3A writing group to hone her gifts as writer and poet. The result was the publication of her first book, a collection of her prose and poems, to mark her ninetieth year.[5] She coupled this endeavour with fundraising by contributing sale proceeds of the book to The Multiple Sclerosis Society in memory of her husband. This is illustrative of how it is never too late to embark on such projects, but they are fulfilled as a result of a willingness to remain engaged with living life.

The Christian should engage with the opportunities that life presents, and to be continually mindful of doing so, remembering the words of St. Paul in his First Letter to the Thessalonians: 'Finally, brothers and sisters, we ask and urge you in the Lord Jesus that, as you learned from us how you ought to live and to please God (as, in fact, you are doing), you should do so more and more.'[6] And we should not overlook that at the end of that letter, St. Paul urges very succinctly 'Beloved, pray for us.'[7]

Nothing exemplifies the opportunity to remain engaged more than the chance to reinvigorate our prayer lives. If we are honest, many of us struggle at times with giving prayer the time it deserves. In later life we can enrich our prayer with the fact that we are free to give it full time and focus. More to the point, prayer is something through which we can remain engaged with the world even though our health may be in decline. It was my privilege at St. John's to know a remarkable woman called Elizabeth. As her health began to fail she moved into one of our nursing homes. There her physical horizons shrank. Her only son lived in Canada so she had few visitors. Deteriorating health gradually confined her to her room, and then to her bed. And so she remained for several years.

Elizabeth faced a seeming shrinking of her ability to relate to the world about her, but for the remarkable fact of her incredibly powerful prayer ministry. There were a host of people and places for whom she prayed, so that she remained someone fully engaged with the world despite her ongoing illness and frailty. I was humbled to discover from a member of the nursing staff that Elizabeth was regularly praying for me. I was at the time embarking on ordination. The realisation that this wonderful old lady was including me regularly in her prayers moved me deeply. I continue to hold her in mind as the perfect example of how we can in fact remain engaged whatever our health or the limitations of old age.

Mother Harriet, founder of the Clewer Sisters, who used to claim to try to do little things for God's glory without letting anyone know, said in later life that she felt that she had done more real work for God while sitting stuck to her chair than in all her busy active years.[8] I rather fancy that the same could be said of Elizabeth in her confinement to bed. Both were examples of the truth that 'the prayers of saints are what swell the sails of the church in her voyage through this troublesome world.'[9]

There is no limit to the potential of engaging with the world about us. There is never an end to what we might have to offer, as Tennyson demonstrates in *Ulysses*:

……. you and I are old;
Old age hath yet his honour and his toil;

Death closes all: but something ere the end,
Some work of noble note may yet be done.[10]

With poetic vision Tennyson sought a noble purpose, but the work yet to be done may be of a more humble nature. In Tanzania the grandmothers of the Hazda hunter-gatherer people are honoured by their community as possessing special skills as foragers, spending more time at it and with greater success than younger women.[11] This is illustrative of older people sharing skills. Too often there has been a tendency to deskill older people in our country, particularly as they move into nursing care. Recent televised experiments where young children carried out activities with nursing home residents showed considerable mutual benefits.[12] Not only did the residents' general well-being improve but the children benefitted. There is huge potential to increase this sort of interaction and allow frailer older people to have a sense of worth out of such activities.

My mother was always someone keen to help others, a quality which led her to train as a nurse at St. Bartholomew's Hospital in London where she was to meet my father. Years later when admitted to a care home in her eighties with Alzheimer's disease, even as her ability to communicate was declining, she was demonstrating something of this urge to help as she sought to assist the staff in tasks such as bed making and care of other residents. Mindful of her qualification as a nurse the staff affectionately nicknamed her 'matron'. I can still smile now at this interaction because it demonstrated my mother's positive engagement with those about her despite the increasing impact of her dementia.

If we acknowledge this attribute of engagement in terms of spiritual gift, then we should see it as about drawing on our full God-given potential. Some say that one of the greatest sins is the unlived life.[13] For as Mark Oakley writes: 'As a Christian, I believe that God has given us all a gift. It is our being. God asks for a gift in return – our becoming, who we become with our being'.[14] One of the profound spiritual voices of the 20th century was Etty Hillesum, a Dutch Jew murdered in Auschwitz at the age of only 29, but whose diaries and letters reveal a maturity beyond her years. Writing amidst the trauma of the Westerbork transit camp set up by the Nazis in occupied Holland she could nevertheless attest to the need to remain engaged with all that confronted her:

> Perhaps my purpose in life is to come to grips with myself, properly to grips with myself, with everything that bothers and tortures me and clamours for inner solution and formulation. For these problems are not just mine alone. And if at the end of a long life I am able to give some form to the chaos inside me, I may well have fulfilled my own small purpose.[15]

Many would attest to the sense of achievement possible at the end of a long life, something which was not to be accorded to Etty Hillesum dying so young. In her eighties Florida Scott-Maxwell was able to look back in these terms:

> If I suffer from my lacks, and I do daily, I also feel elation at what I have become. At times I feel a sort of intoxication because of some small degree of gain; as though the life that is in me has been my charge, the trust birth brought me, and my blunders, sins, the blanks in me as well as the gifts, have in some long painful transmutation made the life that is me clearer.[16]

Just as her meditation on the ageing process displays a real sense of self-knowledge and honesty, it reminds us that being true to ourselves is a great strength, helping us to live out our lives as fully as possible until death.

As I was putting the final touches to this book amidst national lockdown because of the Coronavirus pandemic, the country was taking to its heart 99 year old Captain Tom Moore. His resolve to walk one hundred laps of his garden to raise funds for the National Health Service certainly struck a national chord. His commitment to this cause thrilled people, but perhaps at a fearful time what particularly encouraged us all was seeing someone of such an age showing the way. If ever there was an example of remaining engaged with life Captain Tom was demonstrating this, but so too in a more passive way does Florida Scott-Maxwell counting the small gains of each day and Elizabeth offering up prayers from her nursing home bed, both sharing the spirit of engagement right to the end of life.

Our Christian calling is rooted in the intrinsic charge that Jesus gave us all to seek to build his kingdom. What this chapter has highlighted is the fact that we are all called to fulfil our potential in whatever way we can, all called to kingdom building. We have to resist the temptation to see old age as a time of disengagement. However short our remaining time on earth we need to strive to be part of it. This in turn prepares us for the eternal, for the two are intrinsically linked. As Thomas Merton puts it:

> Can a man cling only to heaven
> And know nothing of earth?
> They are correlative: To know one
> Is to know the other.
> To refuse one
> Is to refuse both.[17]

Old age does not ask that we simply look heavenwards. We draw nearer to that goal if we can apply ourselves to make the very most of God's world and engage with it.

Chapter 8

BLESSING

Then the women said to Naomi, 'Blessed be the Lord, who has not left you this day without next-of-kin, and may his name be renowned in Israel. He shall be to you a restorer of life and a nourisher of your old age.'
[Ruth 4:14-15]

The short Old Testament book of Ruth is a powerful story told with economy of words but real narrative power. Naomi travels to the country of Moab with her husband and sons. Her husband dies and then ten years later the sons also die, although they have by then both married. As a result of her bereavements Naomi resolves to return to her homeland of Judah. Her daughters-in-law Orpah and Ruth offer to go with her but she thanks them, kisses them and urges them to return to their own mothers. Orpah agrees to do so, but Ruth declines to do so, clinging to Naomi with an impassioned commitment.

> Do not press me to leave you
> or to turn back from following you!
> Where you go, I will go;
> where you lodge, I will lodge;
> your people shall be my people,
> and your God my God.
> Where you die, I will die—
> there will I be buried.
> May the LORD do thus and so to me,
> and more as well,
> if even death parts me from you!'[1]

Later Ruth marries and as Naomi acquires new family, a blessing in her old age, local women give thanks in the words that preface this chapter. This always strikes me as a story of mutual blessings, and it ends on this note of thankful acknowledgement of this before God. Earlier in the book there is the implicit blessing by Naomi of her daughters-in-law and then Ruth effectively blesses Naomi as a result of her commitment to stay with Naomi.

An awareness of the intrinsic weave of blessing in our lives is an important ingredient in the spirituality of ageing. Acknowledging life's blessings is a way of acknowledging God at work around us. As the elderly minister John Ames muses in *Gilead* as he thinks on baptism: 'There is a reality in blessing, which I take baptism to be, primarily. It doesn't enhance sacredness, but it acknowledges it, and there is a power in that.'[2] There is indeed a power in acknowledging the blessings which are windows onto the sacred in our lives. This requires though a conscious effort on our part to be open to the transcendent about us.

Finding blessing around us is a path to God, but it is not an easy one as some often quoted words of Gerard Manley Hopkins illustrate.

> I kiss my hand
> To the stars, lovely-asunder
> Starlight, wafting him out of it; and
> Glow, glory in thunder;
> Kiss my hand to the dappled-with-damson west:
> Since, tho' he is under the world's splendour and wonder,
> His mystery must be instressed, stressed;
> For I greet him the days I meet him, and bless when I understand.[3]

Hopkins captures something of the way that we sense that we are blessed without always being able to fully understand the enormity of God's goodness to us. It is not for nothing that Hopkins paints the evocative natural setting where he might find and greet God. There are many writers and poets who would concur that we can take our troubles into a very real encounter with God if we do so. There is a moving passage in Richard Llewellyn's powerful evocation of a Welsh mining village when the narrator Huw Morgan finds peace in the hills:

[I] went out, and up on top of the mountain to have peace, for I
had a grudge that was savage with heart against everybody, and only
up on top there, where it was green, and high, and blue, and quiet,
with only the winds to come at you, was a place of rest, where the
unkindness of man for man could be forgotten, and I could wait for
God to send calm and wisdom, and O, a blessed ease.[4]

An ability to sense God's blessings in this way is but a precursor to
finding God's presence in each other. The ability to do so is part
of the spirituality which strengthens us as we age. There is a rather
endearing story of the nineteenth century Bishop Wordsworth
of Lincoln who was lying dying in his bed. He heard the cry of his
little baby granddaughter in an adjoining room and asked for her to
be brought in to him. Having asked to see her she was brought to
his bedside and her mother asked the Bishop to bless the baby girl
which he did. He then indicated that she must bless him. When he
asked whether she had done so, the mother gently explained that the
baby could not yet speak, but she then guided the baby's hand to his
forehead and indicated that the baby had given the blessing.[5]

Bishop Wordsworth on his death bed was demonstrating that
blessing is a mutual gift, and the more it is used to bind us together
with others the more it unites us with God. My daughter Alice
married into a Polish family. In accordance with a Polish custom, at
her wedding the parents of bride and groom stepped forward to each
bestow a blessing on the newly married couple in their own words.
I found that profoundly moving as one generation blessed the next.

In one of my parishes there were two elderly ladies whom I used to
visit who would both pepper their talk with 'bless him' or 'bless her' as
they talked of people they knew. In some people such expressions can
suggest a sort of forced affectation, but in both these ladies I sensed
a real empathetic concern for those whom they were speaking about.
I always felt that this was a bit more than just a figure of speech like
that modern response when someone tells an endearing story and the
hearer responds 'bless'. You felt they really did want to bless the people
they were talking about. It is a short word and all that is needed to be
transformative in our prayers, as Jim Cotter explains so well:

There is something I find important here about my praying for others. If I can keep alive within me this being expectant of the unexpected, if I experience – both in solitude and in conversation – the gift of that which is new, then there may be a Spirit at work within us and among us that is mostly hidden and which cannot be measured or grasped, but which is having a profound influence upon us. It is into that possibility that I place the names of the ones for whom I have a concern. The word I use is the simple 'Bless...' Nothing more specific. After all, there is nothing more I would wish than that others receive a measure of that abundant life implied by a 'blessing'. And it may be that the fitful, almost perfunctory mention of a name triggers a movement of the Spirit. The cosmic net trembles, vibrating with the whispers of prayer. Why should geography or death impede that communication?[6]

Later life allows the time and space to hold others in mind and prayer in the way that Jim Cotter suggests. Many older people live on their own and a natural pitfall is that this can make one self-centred. Taking others to one's heart is a great counter balance to that tendency. As Florida Scott-Maxwell puts it:

There are many whom I never cease cherishing. I dwell on their troubles, their qualities, their possibilities as though I kept them safe by so doing; as though by understanding them I simplified their lives for them. I live with them every minute. I live by living with them.[7]

I have often found that the people who have impressed me as living lives committed to bestowing blessings on others do not necessarily have everything easy, but nevertheless have the sort of mental attitude which sees life through the prism of God's blessing. I remember visiting an elderly lady whose husband had recently died. Amidst all that she was coping with, she said to me 'I never go to sleep without thinking of five blessings in the day to thank God for'. She then added with a soft smile, 'and you know I always find them'. Here was a practical expression of the catchy American hymn *Count Your Blessings*. Christian Aid has rightly engaged with such an awareness of God's grace with the issue of its forty day calendar encouraging people to count their blessings through Lent. It can prove an effective way of helping us to see our lives in a new light in comparison to others around the world.

A similar ability to interrogate life in this way was expressed to me by a former parishioner whose business had gone bankrupt. He went through a tough time, but the thing which he wanted to emphasise to me as we spoke about this was not the financial hardship but the way in which the kindnesses and support he had received from friends and neighbours had been a profound blessing for which he was truly thankful.

After visiting both these people I left feeling in a way that I had in turn been blessed by coming alongside their positive thinking and their ability to find God's blessings in their lives. In a very real way they were themselves a blessing. For me this ability of some people to seek out the blessings in life whatever life dishes out was exemplified in the autobiographical book published some years ago now by Mary Craig. She detailed in this a life in which she faced some crippling blows. Her second son was born with Hurler Syndrome, rather brutally known at the time of his birth as gargoylism, a rare disease which leaves those affected physically impaired and with severe learning disabilities. In her immediate despair she started helping Sue Ryder in work that Sue Ryder was doing with concentration camp survivors from the Second World War. In this work Mary Craig found the peace and strength to accept what had happened to her. This then helped her meet another significant challenge when her fourth son was born with Down's syndrome. The title of her book was simply *Blessings*.[8]

Interestingly, although in her book Mary Craig very clearly found hope and strength in following Jesus she never mentions the word blessings. The blessings referred to in the title flow from her engagement with the world despite her challenges. In this way she touches on the paradoxical way in which life blesses when we might think there is nothing good to be found. 'Life will bring many misfortunes to you, but it is in them that you will find happiness and you will bless life and make others bless it – which is what matters most', writes Fyodor Dostoyevsky.[9] It is not surprising that this paradox intrigues novelists and poets alike. Many sense the intrinsic hope that exists even when we struggle to find it. W. H Auden was a good example of this. As Richard Harries points out, 'he believed we had a choice between shouting in anger and despair at life or blessing what there is for being. He chose the latter course and made praise and gratitude for the ordinary things of life one of the main themes of his poetry'.[10]

> O look, look in the mirror?
> O look in your distress:
> Life remains a blessing
> Although you cannot bless.[11]

After a friend recently shared with me the pain of her husband's admission to a nursing home with Alzheimer's disease she went on to express thanks for the many kindnesses she had experienced from others during the process. This brought to my mind Edwin Muir's sense that we can experience something positive amidst life's problems that is distinct to our world:

> Strange blessings never in paradise
> Fall from these beclouded skies.[12]

It is true that the themes explored in this chapter apply whatever one's age, but they have a particular resonance as we age. Fullness in later life will be emphasised by a sense of blessing. Bestowing a blessing is not just a preserve of priests. Of course through their ordination they do have a specific corporate and individual authority to bless in God's name, but I firmly believe that we should all be more ready to bring God's blessing to bear on those around us. A long life allows us to distill this truth and share it making it a particular preserve of older people.

The Scattering by Christopher Reid was the first poetry collection to win the prestigious Costa Book of the Year Award. In this book Reid tenderly explores the emotional impact of the death of his wife Lucinda on himself and revisits shared experiences. In one poem he captures very movingly the way in which they blessed each other:

One afternoon, years later, we crossed on the stairs.
Unprompted, you announced, 'I love our house' -
an outburst of the plainest happiness
that the high stairwell
enshrines still.

While the innumerable air kisses
we exchanged in passing
remain suspended to this day,
each one an efficacious blessing.[13]

It is not surprising then that there is a Jewish tradition to recall someone who has died with the words 'may her (or his) memory be for a blessing'.

It is incumbent on us all to be thankful for the blessings which life bestows on us, but there is also in the Christian life a charge to be a blessing to others in the way so exemplified by Ruth. Indeed this has early biblical precedent. In Genesis God says to Abraham 'I will bless you and make your name great so that you will be a blessing'.[14] I find those words very moving. As well as bestowing his blessing, God expects Abraham be a blessing to others. It is quite daunting to reflect on how we might ourselves be a blessing to those about us. It even sounds a little presumptuous, but I want to suggest not. If we seek to live out Jesus' Sermon on the Mount[15] then as we become blessed through God's grace, so we can become a blessing. Old age specifically gives us the time to be present for others in a very unique way. It is never too late to do so. That is a theme which George Eliot explores in her final novel Daniel Deronda where the character Mordecai is described as carrying a blessing inside him.[16]

If we can walk in the steps of Christ then it need not be presumptuous if, like him, we seek to share God's love with those about us. So as we follow Jesus in our later years we can all aspire to be a blessing which in turn brings God's blessing on us. As the Book of Proverbs assures us 'the blessing of the Lord makes us rich'.[17] Indeed in the Celtic tradition this becomes an all embracing prayer:

Bless to me O God
The earth beneath my feet.
Bless to me O God
The path on which I go.
Bless to me O God
The people whom I meet.
O God of all gods
Bless to me my life. Amen.[18]

PART 3

FACING A CERTAIN FUTURE

O God, from my youth you have taught me,
and I still proclaim your wondrous deeds.
So even to old age and grey hairs,
O God, do not forsake me,
until I proclaim your might
to all the generations to come.
[Psalm 71:17-18]

Chapter 9

ACCEPTANCE

May you be made strong with all the strength that comes from his glorious power, and may you be prepared to endure everything with patience.
[Colossians 1:11]

It has been my privilege to know a number of people who have reached that still significant landmark birthday of a hundred. Local journalists have always asked the same question at the celebrations: 'What is it that has helped you reach this milestone?' The replies have been varied and sometimes contradictory, such as no alcohol from one or a regular tipple from another! Two who went on to live the longest always put their longevity down to never having married! One thing I observed about these centenarians during my years at St. John's was that most of those who reached the age of a hundred seemed to have the gift of taking life as it comes. Behind that phrase which borders on cliché is in fact the basis of something which I believe to be one of the great spiritual strengths in ageing.

This chapter is headed relatively neutrally 'Acceptance' but in using that word I mean to capture something of that time tempered ability to absorb all that comes one's way. The centenarians at St. John's to whom I have referred had often faced significant challenges and losses in their lives, such as the remarkable Win whose fiancé was killed in the First World War. Having lost the love of her life she never married and lived to be 106. She morphed her loss into the spiritual strength I want to explore. It is an enduring quality which is recognisable when encountered. It is evident in the justly acclaimed autobiographical book *The Salt Path* by Raynor Winn, in which the author describes facing homelessness and her husband's terminal diagnosis by walking the 630 mile South West Coast Path with him. Towards the end of a journey of self-discovery she is able to acknowledge: 'I was no longer striving, fighting to change the unchangeable, not clenching in anxiety at the life we'd been unable to hold on to, or angry at an authoritarian system too bureaucratic to see the truth. A new season had crept into me, a softer season of acceptance.'[1] Indeed she goes on to head the penultimate chapter in her book 'Accepting'.

Fostering acceptance is achieved as a result of cultivating a range of qualities that include resilience, patience, embracing being as opposed to doing, and humility. Casting our minds back we can recall that the thankfulness explored in chapter 8 and manifested in an awareness of our blessings has a strong link to acceptance, for as Ann Morisy argues 'the practice of gratitude provides the nursery slopes for contemplative ageing'.[2]

Acceptance starts with the old adage about taking the rough with the smooth. But accepting the rough with the smooth is more than a passive act of tolerating the difficult things in life. It has a steelier component which we might term resilience. Life fashions us to be more able to cope with its challenges as we draw on the ways in which we have weathered past storms. St. Paul returns more than once to his own sense of this working out in his life. As he puts it, 'therefore I am content with weaknesses, insults, hardships, persecutions, and calamities for the sake of Christ; for whenever I am weak, then I am strong'.[3] But it is in bearing with the challenges of life that we learn patience as he argues in the words which preface this chapter from the Letter to the Colossians. St. Ignatius Loyola identified the value of this in his *Spiritual Exercises* where he writes 'let him who is in desolation labour to be in patience, which is contrary to the vexations which come to him: and let him think that he will soon be consoled.'[4]

Patience is no easy virtue as Gerard Manley Hopkins made clear when he wrote 'Patience, hard thing!' But having explored the challenges patience may ask us to put up with, he discerns a depth which is an instigator of kindness:

And where is he who more and more distils

Delicious kindness?—He is patient. Patience fills
His crisp combs, and that comes those ways we know.[5]

We touched in chapter 6 on trying to avoid worries becoming a burden. The Church used to uphold the virtue of resignation as a way of coping with the vicissitudes of life. Interestingly however, I read recently that Pope Francis had suggested resignation was not a virtue.[6] His reason was that he felt it dispelled hope. Without wanting to get into a semantic debate about the meaning of words, I can appreciate why resignation was deemed a virtue, but to avoid any negative implications I am opting for my suggestion of the more rounded term of 'acceptance'. Far from preventing hope I think it can be a platform for hope for the future. At its heart is an ability to appreciate and value the present moment.

Finding hope in the present is about relishing and savouring what surrounds us and which otherwise risks being taken for granted. There is a real art in recovering something which children are very good at, namely living for the here and now. And actually that is more difficult to achieve than we credit in a society which places such importance on 'doing'. But old age can give us the opportunity to prioritise 'being' in priority to 'doing'. As that turns on its head the ethos of the cut and thrust world about us, one needs confidence to assert this. We have to learn to disengage from the working life. In a real sense ceasing to be a human 'doer' allows us to recapture genuinely becoming a human 'being'.

If your whole working life has been based on striving and achieving, this change of tempo and outlook can be really hard to accept. It will repay the effort and provides a plateau from which one can set forth into the final phase of life with a greater sense of peace. It can also be a chance to redress the balance of one's earlier life where the priorities may have been wrong. With characteristic honesty Richard Holloway acknowledges this when he reflects 'I wish more of my attention had been spent on the 'here' of my life rather than on the 'elsewhere' I was in pursuit of'.[7]

We live in a society so defined by what we are doing that we need a contrasting opportunity to develop an awareness of who we truly are.

Retirement from the pressures of work offers the opportunity. Henri Nouwen highlights this succinctly. 'Our doing brings success, but our being bears fruit. The great paradox of our lives is that while we are often concerned about what we do, or still can do, we are most likely to be remembered for who we were.'[8]

This attitude of mind was well captured by an 18th century Jesuit priest, Jean-Pierre de Causade who was spiritual director to the Nuns of the Visitation in Nancy. His addresses to the nuns were initially published as *Self-Abandonment to Divine Providence* before being republished using one of his most famous phrases, *The Sacrament of the Present Moment.* This is a phrase which captures a key skill in mastering attentiveness to the here and now, that gift of acceptance whatever we may face.

De Causade told the nuns: 'The present moment holds infinite riches beyond your wildest dreams, but you will only enjoy them to the extent of your faith and love. The more a soul loves, the more it longs, the more it hopes, the more it finds.'[9] He continues later: 'The present moment is like an ambassador announcing the policy of God; the heart declares "Thy will be done", and souls, travelling at full speed never stopping, spread the news far and wide.'[10]

Those who master this skill are notably better able to navigate later life and illuminate the lives of others. It is interesting how people who have this gift stand out. In Jane Austen's Persuasion when the heroine Anne Elliot is struggling emotionally she revisits an old school friend, Mrs. Smith, who is disabled and a widow. To her astonishment she finds someone with just such deep reserves of inner strength. 'Neither the dissipations of the past – and she had lived very much in the world, nor the restrictions of the present; neither sickness nor sorrow seemed to have closed her heart or ruined her spirits.'[11] Anne goes on to ponder Mrs. Smith's inner strength despite being a widow, childless, and without relations to assist, in these words:

> 'How could it be? She watched – observed – reflected - and finally determined that this was not a case of fortitude or of resignation only. A submissive spirit might be patient, a strong understanding would supply resolution, but here was something more; here was that elasticity of mind, that disposition to be comforted, that power of

turning readily from evil to good, and of finding employment which carried her out of herself, which was from Nature alone. It was the choicest gift of Heaven; and Anne viewed her friend as one of those instances in which, by a merciful appointment, it seems designed to counterbalance almost every other want.[12]

Reading that I have a feeling that Austen's Mrs. Smith had mastered not just the ability to take the rough with the smooth but truly to accept the sacrament of the present moment. Quite apart from its loftier benefits, such an approach to later life will probably keep us more relaxed and able to become what William Hazlitt called the 'creature of the moment'.[13] Hazlitt was describing the escape of going on a journey but what struck him most was to be 'clear of all ties', and often later life gifts us just that. Not having to do things at a set time or a set way allows a new freedom. I have had a sneaking admiration for the poet Dannie Abse's elderly Uncle Isidore ever since I first read of him, and whom his nephew celebrated in these terms:

'Uncle Isidore, work?'
My brother had said, 'For decades he did nothing
And he didn't do that till after lunch.'[14]

The benefits of finding the sacrament of the present moment undoubtedly take root in the lives of those who master this approach. Elizabeth whom I introduced in chapter 7 would be a good example. Her powerful prayer life was based on just such an attitude. Elizabeth's acceptance meant that she had discovered what one might call serenity, or in monastic life what was known as 'benignitas', difficult to translate from the Latin but what we might deem peaceful benevolence.[15] This is a gift which allows the ability to meet trials such as ill health with unexpected strength.

As I have suggested, there is often a distinctly accepting attitude of mind in many centenarians which for many is rooted in faith. I particularly like these words of one 101 year old: 'I don't suffer old age because I ignore it: it goes ahead on its own, but I pay little heed to it. The only way to live well in old age is to live it in God.'[16]

In this spirit of acceptance we may indeed recognise ongoing roles we have come to undervalue. Metropolitan Anthony describes his grandmother dropping the crockery she is washing up and bemoaning 'why does God allow me to live now that I am good for nothing – not even capable of washing up?' He comforts her by assuring her that she has something which only she can do. 'Since the world began and until eternity unfolds before us, no-one else was capable of being my grandmother.'[17] So as he emphasises, even those feeling useless in old age can be reminded of the relationships which matter and abide in definitive, eternal value.

Acceptance as I have defined it is also a source of the neglected virtue of humility. Some older people try and live later life through the lens only of their past achievements. They need to learn when to let those go and move forwards comfortable in their ongoing identity. 'The temptation in old age is to say, "I am what I was". But that's only half the truth; until the day I die, I am what I am.' So perceptively writes James Woodward.[18] Learning to accept who we are helps us to share humility in our dealings with others and ultimately with God as the prophet Micah memorably bids us.[19] At the heart of humility is a sense of honesty, not just about those around us but about one's self. Too often perceived as a sign of weakness, humility is at heart a sign of spiritual strength as Thomas Merton suggests.

> Humility consists in being precisely the person you actually are before God, and since no two people are alike, if you have the humility to be yourself you will not be like anyone else in the whole universe. But this individuality will not necessarily assert itself on the surface of everyday life. It will not be a matter of mere appearances, or opinions, or tastes, or ways of doing things. It is something deep in the soul.[20]

Those called to the religious life like Merton often learn how to really mine deep in the soul for humility. The Benedictine nun Sister Mary David also highlights the importance of humility, but crucially suggests how this leads to possibilities for growth, so making this a dynamic rather than passive quality. It allowed her to find what she characterised as 'acceptance-with-joy' even as she faced terminal bowel cancer:

> Accepting reality with all its limitations in oneself and others, being creative with weakness and imperfections, knowing how to use them to grow and deepen: this seems to be what humility is all about. In a mysterious way these difficulties, imperfections, trials, which reveal our weakness are where we find real human life in all its profundity. We learn to live with them, and gradually we realise that they are not as threatening as we thought they were – indeed these things open us up to God's love and power. It is just here that our deepest strength and our possibilities for growth lie hidden.[21]

One of the besetting challenges of later life is to fret over what we have not achieved. Sometimes in humility we have to accept what we might have wished to achieve in life but may no longer be able to. As one character says to another in Patrick Gale's novel *A Perfectly Good Man*, 'might-have-beens are insidious, aren't they, in the way they don't ever quite lie still or go away'.[22] The gift of acceptance gently lets such thoughts fall away. Age allows us to temper regret and meld it into experience. When we start to achieve this we are showing a sense of maturity. Life is messy and we have to accept its imperfections as much as its achievements. 'One sign of maturity is the acceptance – not just the tolerance – of ambiguity'.[23]

Living with ambiguities means acknowledging that we may not always have the answers, but a spirit of acceptance will throw us back on our God given resources and our trust in God. Trust, as we know, is something that needs to be developed, and God is no exception. Perfecting that allows us to place our future in his hands and join with Pádraig Daly in his poem *Prayer in Age*[24]:

> Let me trust You, Lord, to the going-out of my days.

> When I am led again in halterstrings,
> Grant that I be led kindly:
> Do not abandon me to derision.

When nights are dark
And I have no strength, even to pray,
Do not cast me off.

Lead me to those fields
Where every sheep is known by name.
Let me be as rain on your ocean.

Chapter 10

PASSION

I have been crucified with Christ; and it is no longer I who live, but it is Christ who lives in me. And the life I now live in the flesh I live by faith in the Son of God, who loved me and gave himself for me.
[Galatians 2: 19b-20]

Although society today probably understands the word passion most readily as an embodiment of extreme emotion, it has of course a deeper meaning. We speak of passion as the state of being acted upon, even to the extent of suffering. Hence as Christians we talk of the passion of Christ, the events which unfold after his arrest in the garden of Gethsemane. There is a marked contrast between his active ministry and this final period of his life. As the words which preface this chapter remind us, committing ourselves to Christ will mean entering into that passion ourselves. 'We Christians find hope by living inside a story' suggests Timothy Radcliffe [1] and this means we will find ourselves called into Christ's passion just as much as any other part of the story of his life. Such is the consequence of wholehearted commitment to following him.

In W. H. Vanstone's justifiably acclaimed book *The Stature of Waiting* the author explores the dramatic contrast between the period of Jesus' ministry when he is the instigator of so much compared to his last hours when he is the object of the actions of others. Revealingly Vanstone says this of the word passion: 'The word 'passion' does not mean, exclusively or even primarily, 'pain': it means dependence, exposure, waiting, being no longer in control of one's situation, being the object of what is being done.' [2]

Read slowly and reflectively those words summarise so well one of the great fears of ageing: that we will face a period of dependence in contrast to the vigour and activity of our earlier life. Talking to older people, I have found this fear of dependence is one of their greatest fears, united as it is to fear of being in pain and discomfort. Coupled with this is a fear of what being in such a state might do to their nearest and dearest, the fear of not wanting to be a burden. Like all fears these can be disabling and can prompt a vigorous sense of denial which is potentially destructive to the human spirit.

The possibility of dependence on others in later life is not a new phenomenon. Indeed there is a telling biblical indication of this possibility in John's gospel where Jesus says to Simon Peter: 'Very truly, I tell you, when you were younger, you used to fasten your own belt and to go wherever you wished. But when you grow old, you will stretch out your hands and someone else will fasten a belt around you and take you where you do not wish to go.'[3] Pádraig Daly doubtless had this in mind when he wrote the poem with which the previous chapter closed.

One of the qualities of the gift of acceptance explored in that chapter is that we should not let the fear of being dependent paralyse us. We need to remember the example of Jane Austen's Mrs. Smith who would not let sickness nor sorrow close her heart or ruin her spirit. Even more difficult for those who have always prided themselves on being independently-minded is the fear of being no longer in control as they become more dependent on others. On a number of occasions at St. John's I met those who railed against this. There is an art to knowing when to let some of the independence of spirit go, and acknowledge we need help and accept that graciously. If we can do that we can achieve what one writer in her eighties calls 'heroic helplessness'.[4]

Long before Vanstone's reflections on the theology of waiting John Milton had drawn powerfully on a similar theme in his sonnet *On His Blindness*:

> When I consider how my light is spent
> E're half my days, in this dark world and wide,
> And that one Talent which is death to hide,

Lodg'd with me useless, though my Soul more bent
To serve therewith my Maker, and present
My true account, least he returning chide,
Doth God exact day-labour, light deny'd,
I fondly ask; But patience to prevent
That murmur, soon replies, God doth not need
Either man's work or his own gifts, who best
Bear his milde yoak, they serve him best, his State
Is Kingly. Thousands at his bidding speed
And post o're Land and Ocean without rest:
They also serve who only stand and waite.[5]

There is a powerful statement in Milton's poem of the frustration engendered by the uselessness he feels, the inability to be exercising his unspecified talent. It has been suggested that there is an echo of Job's frustration in the first half of the poem, before patience comes to bear towards its end where we find a powerful recognition of the stature of waiting.

For many people a spirit of independence drives them along through tough times and is fiercely defended. Ironically something which can be a great strength can weigh the same person down when it prompts a refusal to face facts and accept help. I acknowledge that for the independently-minded accepting help can be hard. My father found it a real struggle to accept help when my mother's Alzheimer's worsened and then again when his own physical health declined. It was hard, but one of the kindest things I could offer as his son was to explore with him the need to accept that dependence on others was now inevitable.

Not only is it hard for those whose health is declining, but also those who journey with them. After my mother had been admitted to a care home and her mental health severely affected it was a source of great personal pain to observe this, both for me and other members of the family. I guess we all had different coping strategies. For myself I kept a cd of Beethoven's late string quartets in my car and I found great solace in playing the slow movement from Quartet No.16 Opus 135 as I drove home. Beethoven marked this 'Lento assai, cantante e tranquillo', broadly translated as 'very slow indeed, singing and calm'. I am no musician but I understand that my old recording by the Busch Quartet plays this movement unusually slowly. Somehow the music articulated the pain, but having done so plateaued into calm.

In the light of the solace I found in Beethoven's music at this time, I was moved recently to discover that he had himself supported a friend, Dorothea von Ertmann, after the deaths of her children through illness. She subsequently shared with Mendelssohn how Beethoven had been initially unable to visit her after the death of her last child, but then finally invited her to his house. When she came he merely said 'we will now converse in music'. He played for over an hour and as she expressed it, 'he said everything to me, and also finally gave me consolation'.[6] As so often music can encapsulate emotions and can remind us of pain but of a peace beyond. Such is the passion which we may find ourselves entering into during our lives. This can of course occur at any stage, but loss and ill health can accentuate this in old age, either for ourselves or those whom we love.

There is a path of passion in accompanying a loved one as they age. My mother had Alzheimer's disease for well over twelve years, and she spent the last seven years in a nursing home. By the end she was unable to speak and needed everything doing for her, so it was a very hard time for the family. It is indeed a cruel disease. One thing which I encountered a lot during those years was friends and acquaintances asking me a seemingly simple question. 'Does she still know you?' they would ask. I know that this was well meant. They were in a sense empathising with how awful it must be not to be recognised by someone you love. But I came to find this an unhelpful enquiry which grated because I felt it carried a sort of sub-text along the lines of 'I do sympathise because if she doesn't know you then there must be no ongoing relationship'. To that sentiment I wanted to protest 'well actually it doesn't matter because I know her'. I had such knowledge and love of her as to be able to continue to sustain the relationship even if she was unable to articulate that for herself. It was my calling to enter into her passion and be her memory.

One of the profound gifts of the L'Arche communities for people with learning disabilities referred to earlier in chapter 4 is to teach us that we can enter into the passion of each other in ways which grow us in love. The writer and priest Henri Nouwen gave up a successful academic career to join the L'Arche community in Toronto. There he had particular responsibility for the care of one resident called Adam Arnett. Nouwen wrote movingly of Adam in a book entitled *Adam: God's Beloved*, and he devoted a chapter to what he describes as 'Adam's passion'. He shares how Adam lived in total and utter dependency but resigned to it, and he observes:

> Adam's passion for me was a profound prophetic witness. His
> life and especially his passion radically criticised those of us who
> give ourselves to the norms of a society driven by individualism,
> materialism, and sensationalism. Adam's total dependence made it
> possible for him to live fully only if we lived in a loving community
> around him. His great teaching to us was, 'I can live only if you
> surround me with love and if you love one another. Otherwise my life
> is a burden.'[7]

Nouwen reminds us that for significant parts of our lives we are dependent on others, a large part of our lives is passion in which we need others. He concludes:

> We need people, loving and caring people, to sustain us during the
> times of our passion and thus support us to accomplish our mission.
> That, to me, is the final significance of Adam's passion: a radical call
> to accept the truth of our lives and to choose to give our love when
> we are strong and to receive the love of others when we are weak,
> always with tranquillity and generosity.[8]

Those words have a resonance for me in my mother's life. Gentle care giver during her life, she became a total receiver of care from some deeply loving nursing home staff. I was similarly called to enter into her passion. Whatever the ravages of Alzheimer's, I never felt I lost touch with her personhood, however much her mind disintegrated. Like Finuala Dowling who shares in her poetry some of the challenges of her own mother's dementia, I could identify with these words:

Then I think how, at eighty-five,
my mother's mind is a castle in ruin.

Time has raised her drawbridge, lopped her bastions.
Her balustrade is crumbled, and she leans.

Yet still you may walk those ramparts in awe.
Sometimes when she speaks, the ghostly ensign flies.

Time cannot hide what once stood here,
or its glory.[9]

Entering into the passion of later life does not wipe out our identity, just as the worst that Alzheimer's could inflict on my mother did not hide her glory in my eyes. As we learn to accept the process we may come to achieve what Margaret Drabble describes in a sharply observed novel exploring ageing as old age shining with the aura of a lived life.[10] At the heart of an understanding of the passion of old age is an awareness that we can retain our humanity even when we are essentially a recipient of the attentions of others. 'It is not necessarily the case that a man is most fully human when he is achiever rather than receiver, active rather than passive, subject rather than object of what is happening'.[11] So says Vanstone, writing in an era before inclusive language. It is then this passion which is at the heart of the gospel and Jesus' acceptance of this and of its consequences gives us a template for transcending such pain. He also passed from activity and work achievement into a final phase of waiting and dependence, accepting his passion.

In committing ourselves to Christ in our lives we acknowledge that we may have a cross to bear, but one that will unite us with him as the words from the Letter to the Galatians at the beginning of this chapter make clear. There is no glory in pain of itself, but we can be forged anew when we enter our own passion. I am disturbed by some Christians who aspire to celebrate Easter without fully entering into the depths of Good Friday. The two are integral. We cannot understand the amazing reality of the resurrection without having experienced with Christ the desolation of the crucifixion. In a published Good Friday address Michael Mayne says this:

> And God is to be seen in us both in our active, creative lives and in our passivity when that is forced on us, and he will be seen in the spirit in which we accept what others do for us, in how we respond to those on whom we now depend. Those forced to be inactive or to suffer by sickness, handicap or old age must not feel, and must not be made to feel, that they are any less valuable as human beings, or that they do not have a real contribution to make.[12]

Accepting the passion in our lives can lead us into a deeper personal awareness, and certainly an ability to ride the waves which might otherwise overwhelm us in later life. Some learn this at an earlier age through the challenges which they face. Etty Hillesum, whose diaries and letters reveal such remarkable spiritual insight wrote towards the end of her short life:

> I now realise, God, how much you have given me. So much that was beautiful and so much that was hard to bear. Yet whenever I showed myself ready to bear it, the hard was directly transformed into the beautiful. And the beautiful was sometimes much harder to bear, so overpowering did it seem. To think that one small human heart can experience so much, Oh God, so much suffering and so much love.[13]

She was articulating the revelation that we can come closer to God in our times of weakness, something which St. Paul knew well as we saw in the previous chapter. Writing to the Corinthians he tells them that '[the Lord] said to me, "My grace is sufficient for you, for power is made perfect in weakness." So, I will boast all the more gladly of my weaknesses, so that the power of Christ may dwell in me.'[14] Although it is understandable that we fear dependency and the weakness associated with it, we are then at such times very directly linked to Jesus and his passion.

It is part of the great mystery of the spiritual journey that we find ourselves drawing on the times when we were at our lowest. As Jonathan Sachs writes:

There are times when the veil that covers the surface of events lifts, and we catch a glimpse of the larger pattern of which unknowingly, we have been a part. Tradition calls this Divine providence, and I believe in it. Later events make sense of earlier ones. Bad things turn out to have been necessary steps in an important journey.[15]

One of the great attempts to synthesise the working of divine providence is to be found in *Le Milieu Divin* by the Jesuit priest Teilhard de Chardin. It contains for me one of the post powerful expressions of the passion into which we may all be drawn, and rather than seeing this as an experience which separates us from God, locates God within that very process. I first came across the passage as having been personally chosen by Bishop John Robinson for his memorial Service at Trinity College Cambridge. Years later it was to be my privilege to read this at the funeral of Professor Terence Morris which he had similarly chosen in advance. Teilhard de Chardin addresses God in these words:

After having perceived You as He who is 'a greater myself', grant, when my hour comes, that I may recognise You under the species of each alien or hostile force that seems bent upon destroying or uprooting me. When the signs of age begin to mark my body (and still more when they touch my mind); when the ill that is to diminish me or carry me off strikes from without or is born within me; when the painful moment comes in which I suddenly awaken to the fact that I am ill or growing old; and above all at that last moment when I feel I am losing hold of myself and am absolutely passive within the hands of the great unknown forces that have formed me; in all those dark moments, O God, grant that I may understand that it is You (provided only my faith is strong enough) who are painfully parting the fibres of my being in order to penetrate to the very marrow of my substance and bear me away within Yourself.[16]

Chapter 11

DEATH

The last enemy to be destroyed is death.
[1 Corinthians 15:26]

When I first began to reflect on the possibility of writing this book I took a sabbatical from my work at St. John's and went away for a few weeks. I had only begun the process when I received word that my ninety year old father who had been very frail had taken a turn for the worse. I packed up and returned home so as to be nearer to him and the writing of the book went on hold. A few days later I spent the final day of his life at his bedside in the nursing home where he had been living, and I was holding his hand as he died. He had had a period of discomfort earlier in the week but was pain free as he died.

Some while beforehand I had asked him whether he feared dying. He assured me that he did not, and I believe that was indeed the case. As a doctor he had himself seen many people die, so he was fully conversant with the physical process of death. When he died there was a deep sense of peace; so much so that I had to call the nursing home staff to be sure that he had indeed died. It was a death that is at the end far more common than we sometimes imagine. It echoed that of Minnie in Pádraig Daly's poem of the same name.

> Like a boat, serenely, on a sea after storm,
> When the sun newly lights the waters,
> You lie in your hospital bed,
> Grateful to the nurses,
> Reaching to grasp our hands,
> Slipping gently into God.[1]

He had struggled with increasing frailty through the final three years of his life, and sad though I was to see him die, I knew that he was ready to go. However serene or otherwise our final hours, there comes a moment when in Daly's beautiful phrase we do indeed slip gently into God. There was a profound sense of completion to a long and full life when my father died. He would have approved of the GP who gave as cause of death on his death certificate just two words, 'old age', which gave his life a sense of natural completion.

As it happened, Easter fell only a fortnight later, and during Holy Week I was able to reflect on my loss during the marking of the passion and death of Jesus. I was aided in doing so by going to a performance of Simon McEnery's wonderfully evocative oratorio *The Resurrection*. Much of the music we listen to during Holy Week explores the path to the cross but this is a work which moves forwards from the cross. It begins where another often performed oratorio John Stainer's *Crucifixion* ends with Jesus' final words on the cross 'consummatum est....it is finished'.[2] Within that phrase from John's gospel there is so much compressed meaning which Jeremy Davies' text for *The Resurrection* makes beautifully clear: 'It's finished, it's completed, it's perfected'.

Those words seem to me to be a powerful goal for us all as we contemplate death, but they require an acknowledgement from us of the inevitability of death. There is a worrying trend today in the fact that the advances of medicine can give some people an illusory feeling that death can be for ever postponed; what has been expressively described as a culture of 'medical immortality'.[3] I have witnessed sons and daughters of clearly dying parents repeatedly denying the inevitability of that outcome to the detriment of all involved.

What I am highlighting here is not just the knowledge of the inevitable, but more importantly of accepting it, accepting that our lives must finish. Freud argued that we should make friends with the necessity of dying.[4] In a society where people struggle with talking openly of death and dying this is not easy. In the past this may well have been made less easy by seemingly unreal suggestions from the Church, such as the lines in an old hymn 'Teach me to live, that I may dread/ the grave as little as my bed'.[5] It was my experience at St John's that many older people would like to articulate their hopes and fears about dying, but we need to allow space and permission for that to take place. Finding peace at the prospect of your own death can give you renewed ability to live, or as Rabbi Harold Kushner puts it: 'It is only when you are no longer afraid to die that you can say that you are truly alive.'[6]

Etty Hillesum, whose spiritual insight I have already shared, worked in a transit camp for Jews who were to be deported to Auschwitz before the same fate befell her. She seemed to master this balancing of death with life. Living daily with the fear of death as she did, she was still remarkably able to translate that into a positive perspective in her diary:

> By coming to terms with life I mean: the reality of death has become a definite part of my life; my life has, so to speak, been extended by death, by my looking death in the eye and accepting it, by accepting destruction as part of life and no longer wasting my energies on fear of death or the refusal to acknowledge its inevitability. It sounds paradoxical: by excluding death from our life we cannot live a full death, and by admitting death into our life we enlarge and enrich it.[7]

Finding in ourselves the gift of not being afraid can unlock a more rounded sense of the ending of our lives, not just that they are finished, but completed. This gives a fullness to what we may be achieving as we face the inevitable. As we grow older we are inevitably drawing closer to the moment of completion of our earthly lives. It is the knowledge of this which in one sense makes the spiritual exploration of later life a 'spirituality of completion.'[8]

The idea of working at how we might die is rather well illustrated by the story told of Archbishop Geoffrey Fisher who was being fussed over by his wife as he lay in bed, and remonstrated with her 'Don't bother me, dear, I'm busy dying'![9] Certainly a spirituality of completion may help some to experience a peaceful end. Another gentle episcopal story can be found in Anthony Trollope's *Barchester Towers* when the death of Bishop Grantly occurs, so unlocking the machinations explored in the novel: 'Bishop Grantly died as he had

lived, peaceably, slowly, without pain and without excitement.....
Nothing could be easier than the old man's passage from this world.'[10]

It is important to acknowledge that many feel fear not so much
at death itself but at the possible manner of it. We know that we
cannot all slip quite as gently from this world as Bishop Grantly or
my father. The possibility of pain, paralysis or loss of mental faculties
are understandably present for many. There is no simple path which
determines how we might prepare ourselves for such fears. Our ability
to do so will however be rooted in the way in which we are able to
draw on some of the gifts already explored.

There is a lovely passage in the Old Testament book of Genesis.
Jacob who has for some time believed that his youngest son Joseph is
dead learns that Joseph is in fact alive and prospering in Egypt. Jacob
announces to Joseph's brothers who have brought this news 'My son
Joseph is still alive. I must go and see him before I die.'[11] Those words
touch on two key things; firstly the need to be in touch with our own
mortality and secondly preparing ourselves, doing what needs to be
done before we die.

The first task is to cultivate a healthy acknowledgement of our
own mortality. This is not easy in a society which struggles to be
open about the subject. The reasons for this are varied. 'Death is
not so much distanced as sanitized or domesticated, made part of
the spectrum of consumer choice in a consumer society' suggests
Diarmaid Macculloch.[12] He makes a telling point, and this is typified
by attempts to avoid the word and substitute euphemisms such as
'passing away'. There is an aversion nowadays to being honest about
the fact of death. The willingness to allow increasing medicalisation
of death has removed it from daily experience in much of our western
world. Modern medical practice has played a significant part in
this with its tendency to move people to hospital to die despite not
always being prepared for that role with the notable exception of
the hospice movement. As the 2014 Reith lecturer Atul Gawande
points out: 'Medical professionals concentrate on repair of health,
not sustenance of the soul. Yet – and this is the painful paradox – we
have decided that they should be the ones who largely define how we
live our waning years'.[13] Despite this, as one palliative care physician

has acknowledged 'there is a distinct medical unease with, and shying away from, the ubiquitous business of human dying'.[14]

Woody Allen once memorably wrote: 'I'm not afraid of dying. I just don't want to be there when it happens.' That makes us smile but reminds us of our difficulty in confronting the inevitability of death. Diarmaid MacCulloch goes on from the comments above to highlight how the Church has lost its preeminent role in articulating society's response to death. It is true that in an increasingly secular society people do not necessarily look to the Church for this guidance, but I believe it is important that the Church does not abandon a commitment to framing how we should approach dying. It is a particular charge to priests at their ordination that they are to minister to the sick and prepare the dying for death. This is both privilege and responsibility which I have valued highly in my ministry; but it is also right that we should all help each other to prepare for death.

Ask many people today about how they might wish to die and they will indicate in reply that they hope to die quickly and not knowing anything about it. Look, however, at the Litany in the Book of Common Prayer and we find there that it specifically includes a petition that we might be spared sudden death. The fear of sudden death was rooted in a wish to be able to prepare oneself for death. For example in the Victorian era when death was so much more of an experience in families a good death was deemed to be when you might summon your family around you and say your farewells. This might be characterised as 'fully conscious, in the midst of loved ones, well prepared, all the important things having been said beforehand'.[15] For example, Queen Victoria recorded in her journal that Lord Tennyson's death was 'a worthy end' as he 'died with his hand on his Shakespeare and the moon shining full into the window over him'. Reflecting on the Queen's journal entry the poet U. A. Fanthorpe highlights this sense of preparedness:

Our fathers were good at dying.
They did it lingeringly,
As if they liked it; correctly,
With earnest attention to detail,

Codicils brought up to date,
Forgiveness, confession, last-gasp
Penitence properly witnessed
By responsible persons. Attorneys,
Clerics, physicians, all knew their place
In the civil pavane of dying.[16]

Spiritual preparedness is helped by starting with practical steps that acknowledge both decline of health and the inevitability of dying. The act of preparing a power of attorney and writing a will is an act of engagement, so too is giving some thought to what one might wish for one's funeral. The detail and extent of this may vary with the family. I have ministered to some newly bereaved who have been relieved to have been left a complete order of service by their deceased loved one. I do believe though that crafting a service is a very cathartic first step in bereavement. When one of my daughters wrote to urge me to put down some thoughts for myself, I decide to give a range of possibilities. That way the family will have an awareness of my ideas but will need to select and organise. This ensures they will have a clear role in preparing for the funeral and truly own it.

Another powerful act of preparation lies in articulating thanks to those we love and who matter to us. The importance of this was brought home to me when a good friend of mine was dying of cancer. There came a moment when she was admitted to hospital, not necessarily permanently but for treatment. I visited and was about to leave when I felt prompted to say how much our friendship had meant to me and she took the cue to respond similarly. On the way back to the car I was troubled lest this might have been misinterpreted as my implying that she was about to die. That was not the case and she lived for a while afterwards, but by the time I saw her again she was very ill and such a conversation was not possible. It taught me the importance of speaking gratitude and appreciation to others, and not postponing such words lest death prevents them being said.

Having long felt the importance of this, I was interested to read recently that Cardinal John Henry Newman came to acknowledge the importance of expressing appreciation to friends. His special friendship with Father Ambrose St. John was acknowledged during his lifetime but it is clear Newman failed to fully articulate what he felt before St. John's early death. Years later Newman wrote to another friend Sister Maria Pia to thank her, mindful of not having done so to St. John: 'Since his death, I have been reproaching myself for not expressing to *him* how much I felt *his* love – and I write this lest I should feel the same about you, should it be God's will that I should outlive you.'[17] Perhaps the best expression of this aspect of preparation for death comes in W. H. Auden's famous line 'Let your last thinks all be thanks.'[18]

Poignant evidence of the desirability of acknowledging our mortality and preparing for death came in an internet blog which was viewed by three million people in its first year and subsequently published as a book, *The Top Five Regrets of the Dying*. The author Bronnie Ware's experience as a carer of the dying suggested these were, in summary: 'I wish I'd had the courage to live a life true to myself, not the life others expected of me; I wish I hadn't worked so hard; I wish I'd had the courage to express my feelings; I wish I had stayed in touch with my friends; and finally, I wish I had let myself be happier.'[19] I find these expressed regrets sad because they evidence unhappy deaths. I want to affirm in contrast the ways in which I have tried to suggest that a coherent spirituality will in later life allow us to approach death without such overwhelming feelings of regret.

I do not underestimate the challenge of facing what St. Paul describes in the quotation prefacing this chapter as the last enemy. But viewing death simply as an enemy to be held at bay will always result in defeat. Dylan Thomas' famous poem *Do not go gentle into that good night*[20] is understandably popular and features in many anthologies of poetry for funerals. His repeated refrain 'rage, rage, against the dying of the light' is perhaps more an expression of the pain of the bereaved than what I believe we should wish for ourselves as death approaches. That said, few of us may be able to emulate Cicely Saunders in the opposite extreme. I was told of a visitor to the dying Dame Cicely, committed Christian and founder of the hospice movement, who was surprised to be told that she was so excited at her imminent death and the life that lay beyond!

For most of us we face death with varying degrees of trepidation, but the more we have engaged with its inevitability the more we shall be able to begin a process of detachment, a readiness. This at least allows us to join with Kent in *King Lear* in saying 'I have a journey, sir, shortly to go. My master calls me. I must not say no.'[21] That idea of a journey to embark upon has appealed to many. Francis de Sales on the other hand compared preparing for death to transplanting a tree. If one wants to transplant a tree to another soil, one must dexterously disengage each little root one after another, and since we are about to be transplanted from this world in death, we must withdraw our affections from the earth.[22] It is has often been observed that there are many 'last moments' as we age, the last time of doing things or last experiences. Rather than regretting these we should accept them as steps on the journey or as de Sales suggests a process of beginning to disengage our roots ahead of death.

St. Paul's highlighting of death as the final enemy is made so that he can unpack the transformative power of the gospel shared by Christ which assures us of the defeat of death with the promise of eternal life. The more we have rooted our spirit in love and compassion for others the more it will have prepared us, which is a theme he argues elsewhere: 'To those who by patiently doing good seek for glory and honour and immortality, he will give eternal life'.[23] It is my firm belief that all that we have explored hitherto gives us a basis for having confidence in our ability to face the 'last enemy' with confidence and the hope with which I want to close in the final chapter.

Chapter 12

RESURRECTION

*I want to know Christ and the power of his resurrection and the
sharing of his sufferings by becoming like him in his death, if somehow
I may attain the resurrection from the dead.*
[Philippians 3:10]

There are many books on ageing which conclude with the subject
matter of my previous chapter, the facing and embracing of death.
As I indicated at the outset, however, this study is set firmly within a
Christian context where the aspiration expressed in the words above
from the Letter to the Philippians give us an abiding hope of new life
in Christ with God. By its very nature this is a prospect too wide for
our full understanding, and yet it is right that we celebrate the hope
which Jesus' resurrection gives us all. As physicist and priest John
Polkinghorne puts it, 'it is a perfectly coherent hope that the pattern
which is me will be remembered by God and...will be recreated by him
when he reconstitutes me in the new environment of his choosing.'[1]
Many have found this ultimate Christian hope epitomised in the
famous lines of John Donne's Holy Sonnet X:

> One short sleep past, we wake eternally,
> And death shall be no more; death, thou shalt die.[2]

What it might mean to 'wake eternally' is for many compressed into
the words of Jesus often used at funerals that 'in my father's house
there are many dwelling places'.[3] This is cemented in the mind by his
assurance that he goes before us to prepare a place. Somehow that
encapsulates the hope of heaven where we may meet those whom we

have loved. The hope of a link with those who have died is a hope which even elderly agnostics can acknowledge as Richard Hoggart honestly attests in reflecting on later life: 'The oddest surprise of all is that you, an agnostic, still have a slight but ineradicable feeling that those who have "gone before", especially those from whom you tried to learn, are still watching, sometimes shaking their heads.'[4]

The difficulty of positing the nature of resurrection should not prevent us acknowledging it as a reality which touches us as we seek to live lives that follow Jesus as best we can. We begin then to see things from the perspective of the eternal, for which theologians coined the Latin phrase 'sub specie aeternitatis'. There are those whose lives illuminate ours in such a way as to give a glimpse of the eternal. Talking of one of the nuns in his study of a convent of nuns David Snowdon writes of one nun, 'Maria already lived partly in heaven'.[5] Maria was a pointer to the eternal. I have been blessed in knowing many older people whose lives have pointed similarly. There are moments when we glimpse eternity and as Carole Bailey Stoneking suggests, 'earthly time becomes a mere shadow of eternity'.[6]

Much of what the Bible highlights can be comprised in one word, remembrance, from the Jewish exodus through to the last supper, and that frames our future. We remember God working through history in all his acts of love. And it is us, small and frail though we are, who become agents of that love. The act of loving another is the most creative force at work in the world. It is my firm belief that we are moving into God's eternal purposes through that love. As the medieval mystic Meister Eckhart put it: 'People who dwell in God dwell in the eternal now.'[7] The love we have shared during our lives sets us in the context of eternity. It is vital that we grasp this essential truth which is at the heart of St. John's gospel. Emily Dickinson portrays the link in a wonderfully evocative way:

> The Love a Life can show Below
> Is but a filament, I know,
> Of that diviner thing
> That faints upon the face of Noon -
> And smites the Tinder in the Sun -

And hinders Gabriel's Wing -

'Tis this - in Music - hints and sways -
And far abroad on Summer days -
Distils uncertain pain -
'Tis this enamors in the East -
And tints the Transit in the West
With harrowing Iodine -

'Tis this - invites - appalls - endows -
Flits - glimmers - proves - dissolves -
Returns - suggests - convicts - enchants -
Then - flings in Paradise -[8]

I have always been impressed by the honesty of Rembrandt's unflinching self-portraits as he aged. They somehow capture the decline and frailties of his body whilst at the same time preserving a sense of undimmed personhood. An extract from Elizabeth Jennings' poem *Rembrandt's Late Self-Portraits* is set out on the dedication page to this book and merits rereading at this point. Like the paintings she captures something of the ultimate triumph of old age in being able to say there:

....Your face is bruised and hurt
But there is still love left.[9]

It is my great hope that those who read this book may recognise the gifts of their lives and above all the love still available to share. In an echo of Jennings' poem R. S. Thomas penned a lovely line when he wrote 'over love's depths only the surface is wrinkled'.[10] One of the great achievements of the spiritual life is to have developed such depths despite the ageing process. To do so is very much at the heart of the Christian journey. We are given an assurance over how love endures in the short sentence compressed within St. Paul's great homily to love in chapter 13 of the First Letter to the Corinthians: 'Love never ends.'[11] The great Christian truth which Jesus shares is that we find God in love. 'God is love, and those who abide in love, abide in God, and God abides in them.'[12] Living in love puts us on the path to eternity. Thomas Merton shares a typically powerful reminder of this truth:

> But Love laughs at the end of the world because Love is the door to eternity. He who loves is playing on the doorstep of eternity, and before anything can happen, Love will have drawn him over the sill and closed the door.[13]

In assuring us of resurrection with him, Jesus shared an abiding hope, but its actual process and reality is a concept with which we understandably struggle. We need to have faith and trust nevertheless in his promise of that resurrected existence. And it is in the knowledge that the love we shared with those who have died is a force that unites us with God that we can experience a sense of the truth of the resurrection. John Austin Baker put it so well in these words:

> I rest on God who will assuredly not allow me to find the meaning of life in his love and forgiveness, to be wholly dependent on him for the gift of myself, and then destroy that meaning, revoke the gift. He who holds me in existence now can and will hold me in it still, through and beyond the dissolution of my mortal frame. For this is the essence of love, to affirm the right of the beloved to exist. And what God affirms, nothing and no-one can contradict.[14]

Having had the privilege to know Bishop Baker a little, I feel confident that he would have enjoyed as indicative of his faith the words of a letter written in 1884 by a Mgr. Gay who spoke of old age with 'its bodyguard of pains' in words shared by George Congreve:

> For me more than for you, old age has come. May I tell you? I cannot write this word without feeling a smile of sweet surprise in my soul.... I feel so young inwardly; so young that it is almost like childhood. Of course I realize that I have been a traveller for many years on the earth and have seen many things. That makes one thoughtful, grave

sometimes, sometimes sad; one is ripe, one has gained experience; yes, but what is the fruit of all that? It is just a greater evidence that God is all in all, that I am very near my last end, that time is almost nothing, and reality is the spiritual life, that is eternal life has already begun. So clear is this evidence that one feels altogether free, altogether detached, full of energy, ready to spring upward, full of agility to get through the difficulties, full of quietness to let go what is going, filled through and through, in short with God : and this is just old age!'[15]

Ultimately I believe that the spirituality of ageing which I have been exploring in this book centres on recognising the love of God as the force which gives meaning to our lives. The quest for meaning is one of the elusive goals of ageing. Reflection on the richness and diversity of our individual stories in later life will reveal that the weave in the tapestry of those stories is that abiding love, even though at times we struggle to be aware of this. That helpful image of our lives as a tapestry where only God can see the whole picture has been used by many different people, and is well known in a popular anonymous poem, *My Life is but a Weaving* sometimes attributed to Corrie Ten Boom but most likely penned by someone else.

> My life is but a weaving
> Between my God and me.
> I cannot choose the colours
> He weaveth steadily.
> Oft' times He weaveth sorrow;
> And I in foolish pride
> Forget He sees the upper
> And I the underside.
> Not 'til the loom is silent
> And the shuttles cease to fly
> Will God unroll the canvas
> And reveal the reason why.[16]

Helping to reassure people of the weave of God in their lives is an important part of the pastoral care of those who are nearing the end of their lives. There can be an inability to make sense of the past and as we have considered, sometimes regret at the unfulfilled. Yet the image of God as a weaver is as comforting as the Old Testament idea of God moulding us like a potter. Both are offering a sense of God as being bound up in the task of shaping us. This allows us to pray in Ann Lewin's words:

Weaver God, pick up the
Threads of my experience,
Craft the pattern, and
In your time
Reveal significance.[17]

Those words crystallise our quest for meaning. When he died Hermann Melville had arranged for a simple gravestone with his name, date of birth and date of death. Above this was an extravagantly empty scroll which he had chosen as his memorial.[18] The blankness of this it has been suggested seemed to mock all the books he did not write. I find that poignant. Nobody should die with a sense of having lived a life that merits an empty scroll. We are not always the best judges of the significance of our own lives.

We can be our own worse critics sometimes and fail to see the wood for the trees when we look back on our lives. Regrets about the past and unfulfilled dreams should not expunge the achievements wrought, however difficult these may have been in the face of the losses and challenges of a long life. I highlighted the importance of story in Chapter 1 and it is a fundamental of the Christian message that our story is wrapped up in the story of hope shared by Jesus. Charles Pinches in words which should be translated into gender inclusive terms writes this:

For the Christian, however, "preparing for death" does not involve merely loping toward the inevitable moment of expiration. Nor is it a matter simply of settling one's affairs. And the reason it is not merely this lies in Christian hope. Like Simeon, what the Christian looks for when death comes is a vision not of completeness of his own life but of the story by which his life has been borne up. And this he can only know in hope'[19]

I have greatly valued an alternative image of how the threads of our life will be pulled together by God in eternity which is shared in the novel *One Foot in Eden* by Alan Wilkinson. The book tells the life story of Peter, who is a monk and priest. His goddaughter Sue, who is also a priest, having taken his funeral and requiem returns to her parish where she realises she needs to prepare a sermon for the Sunday. She looks up the readings and discovers that the gospel is about Jesus feeding the 5,000. One phrase in this jumps out at her: 'Gather up the fragments left over, so that nothing may be lost.'[20] In her sermon she shares something of her personal loss at the death of her godfather and goes on to say:

> We long to make sense of our lives and the lives of those we love, but our lives often seem a collection of unconnected bits and pieces, like jigsaws with important pieces missing. Was the life of Jesus a bit like that? A healing here, a teaching there, one woman called, another man refusing to respond. Bits and pieces. But in the resurrection all those bits and pieces were gathered together into a seamless whole. Perhaps he will do that for us, and for those we love. For Jesus says about us, as he said about the scraps left on the grass after the feeding, to gather up the fragments left over, so that nothing may be lost.[21]

I find this an enormously helpful insight into how we might view resurrection. God will be the judge of our lives, and however insignificant they may seem the fragments of our life will be taken up and form part of God's eternity. This helps me to surrender my story in the final analysis to God, imperfect as it may seem, in the hope that it will be fashioned into a small part of his eternity. It also means surrendering the brokenness. Those who like my mother have died having lost voice and mind during their earthly life will be re-membered by God. In the Christian promise of the resurrection we have an inkling of the prism through which the God of love sets our

lives into the context of his eternity. Not surprisingly we have to turn
to poetry to capture the enormity of this, and I for one cherish priest
and poet David Scott's typically succinct way of doing so:

...Resurrection is the glass
Through which we see things differently,
And what was first in the mind of God
Becomes the truth at last.[22]

I have in this book considered a range of different perspectives
through which we can view old age. It began with the moulding of our
lives and the way in which that bedrock serves to give us a stability.
It has celebrated the sacrament of the present moment and the gifts
which we find to engage with the present. Finally, it has been shaped
by the hope that we can look into the future with strength of purpose
and the goal of peace. In doing so I want to conclude with a sense of
fulfilment as we look towards the moment when we slip gently into
God and touch at last on the eternal. In doing so we can agree with
Robin Daniels:

The eternal is a like a rainbow: arched over the earth, and yet also
touching, blessing the world of time. The timeless – if only we can
let go, and open ourselves to receive – can heal our past, make our
present rich and full, and give hope for what is to come.[23]

My parting words to you the reader is my great hope that as you lay
down these reflections of mine you will have firmly reminded yourself
of the love of God which guides you, have hope in your heart for what
is to come and, most important of all, still have love left in your heart.

BIBLIOGRAPHY

*[This list shares details of books and papers which have particularly
informed my own reflections and thinking on the themes in this book, but
does not include every source which I have cited in the endnotes.]*

Abse, Dannie, *The Presence* (London: Hutchinson, 2007)

Abse, Dannie, *Two for Joy: Scenes from Married Life* (London:
Hutchinson, 2010)

Albans, Keith, & Johnson, Malcolm, eds., *God, Me and Being Very Old:
Stories and Spirituality in Later Life* (London: SCM Press, 2013)

Albom, Mitch, *Tuesdays with Morrie: An Old Man, A Young Man, and
Life's Greatest Lesson* (London: Time Warner, 1998)

Appleton, George, *Light of Faith: Reflections on Growing Old* (Derby:
Christian Council on Ageing, Occasional Paper No. 9, 1995)

Athill, Diana, *Somewhere Towards the End* (London: Granta, 2008)

Atwell, Robert, *The Contented Life: Spirituality and the Gift of Years*
(Norwich: Canterbury Press, 2011)

Anthony of Sourozh, Metropolitan, *The Spirituality of Old Age* (Derby:
Christian Council on Ageing, Occasional Paper 4, 1993)

Augustine of Hippo, *Confessions,* trans. F. J. Sheed (London: Sheed &
Ward, 1994)

Baker, John Austin, *The Foolishness of God* (London: Darton, Longman
& Todd, 1970)

Barnes, Julian, *Nothing to be Frightened of* (London: Vintage, 2009)

Barry, Sebastian, *Annie Dunne* (London: Faber & Faber, 2002)

Barry, Sebastian, *The Secret Scripture* (London: Faber & Faber, 2008)

Barry, Sebastian, *On Canaan's Side* (London: Faber & Faber, 2011)

Berger Willem, *The Last Achievement* (London: The Grail, 1974)

Blythe Ronald, *The View in Winter: Reflections on Old Age* (London:
Penguin, 1981)

Booth, Wayne, ed., *The Art of Growing Older: Writers on Living and
Aging* (Chicago: University of Chicago, 1982)

Cassidy, Sheila, *Sharing the Darkness: The Spirituality of Caring*
(London: Darton, Longman & Todd, 1988)

Cassidy, Sheila, *Good Friday People* (London: Darton, Longman & Todd, 1991)

Cassidy, Sheila, *Light from the Dark Valley: Reflections on Suffering and the Care of the Dying* (London: Darton, Longman & Todd, 1994)

Chittister OSB, Joan, *The Gift of Years: Growing Older Gracefully* (London: Darton Longman & Todd, 2008)

Congreve SSJE, George, *Treasures of Hope for the Evening of Life* (London: Longmans Green & Co, 1920)

Craig, Mary, *Blessings* (London: Hodder & Stoughton, 1979)

Craig, Mary, *The Last Freedom* (London: Hodder & Stoughton, 1997)

Daly, Pádraig J., *The Other Sea* (Dublin: Dedalus Press, 2003)

Daly, Pádraig J., *Clinging to the Myth* (Dublin: Dedalus Press, 2007)

Daly, Pádraig J., *The Lost Dreamers: New and Selected Poems* (Dublin: Dedalus Press, 2008)

Daly, Pádraig J., *God in Winter* (Dublin: Dedalus Press, 2015)

Daniels, Robin, (ed. Katherine Daniels) *The Virgin Eye: Towards a Contemplative View of Life,* (Watford: Instant Apostle, 2016)

Robert Davis, *My Journey into Alzheimer's Disease* (Amersham: Scripture Press, 1993)

De Caussade, Jean-Pierre, *The Sacrament of the Present Moment,* trans. Kitty Muggeridge (New York: Harper Collins, 1989)

Dowling, Finuala, *Notes from the Dementia Ward* (Cape Town: Kwela Books, 2009)

Drabble, Margaret, *The Dark Flood Rises* (Edinburgh: Canongate, 2016)

Dunmore, Helen, *Inside the Wave* (Hexham: Bloodaxe Books, 2017)

Eger, Edith, *The Choice* (London: Rider, 2017)

Eliot, T. S., *Collected Poems 1909-1962* (London: Faber and Faber, 1974)

Episcopal Society for Ministry on Aging, ed., *Affirmative Aging: A Resource for Ministry* (Minneapolis: Winston Press, 1985)

Frankl, Viktor E., *Man's Search for Meaning* (New York: Washington Square Press, 1985)

Gawande, Atul, *Being Mortal: Illness, Medicine, and What Matters in the End* (London: Profile, 2014)

Goldsmith, Malcolm, *Hearing the Voice of People with Dementia: Opportunities and Obstacles* (London: Jessica Kingsley, 1996)

Goldsmith, Malcolm, *In a Strange Land: People with Dementia and the Local Church* (Southwell: 4M Publications, 2004)

Guenther, Margaret, *Holy Listening: The Art of Spiritual Direction* (London: Darton Longman and Todd, 1982)

Guenther, Margaret, *Toward Holy Ground: Spiritual Directions for the Second Half of Life* (London: Darton Longman and Todd, 1996)

Hare Duke, Michael, *One Foot in Heaven: Growing Older and Living to the Full* (London: SPCK, 2001)

Harries, Richard, *Haunted by Christ: Modern Writers and the Struggle for Faith* (London: SPCK, 2018)

Harris, Jeffrey, *The Great Pilgrimage of Discovery* (Derby: Christian Council on Ageing, Occasional Paper No. 10, 1996)

Hauerwas, Stanley, et al, eds., *Growing Old in Christ* (Grand Rapids: William B. Eerdmans, 2003)

Hawley, Graham, & Jewell, Albert, *Crying in the Wilderness: Giving Voice to Older people in the Church* (Derby: MHA, 2009)

Herbert, George, *Selected Poems* (London: Bloomsbury, 1997)

Hillesum, Etty, *A Diary 1941-43*, (London: Triad Grafton Books, 1985)

Hodgetts, Anthony, *What Next? A Meditation on the Four Last Things* (Derby: Christian Council on Ageing, Occasional Paper No. 12, 2000)

Hoggart, Richard, *Promises to Keep: Thoughts in Old Age* (London: Continuum, 2005)

Holloway, Richard, *Waiting for the Last Bus: Reflections on Life and Death*, (Edinburgh: Canongate, 2018)

Hopkins SJ, Gerard Manley, *Poems*, eds. W.H. Gardner & N. H. MacKenzie (Oxford: Oxford University Press, 1967)

Howse, Kenneth, Religion, *Spirituality and Older People* (London: Centre for Policy on Ageing, 1999)

Jeffery, Peter, *Going Against the Stream: Ethical Aspects of Ageing and Care* (Leominster: Gracewing, 2001)

Jennings, Elizabeth, *The Collected Poems,* ed. Emma Mason (Manchester: Carcanet, 2014)

Jewell, Albert, ed., *Spirituality and Ageing* (London: Jessica Kingsley, 1999)

Jewell, Albert, ed., *Older People and the Church* (Peterborough: Methodist Publishing House, 2001)

Jewell, Albert, ed., *Ageing, Spirituality and Well-being* (London: Jessica Kingsley, 2004)

Johnson, Malcolm, *Committed to the Asylum? The Long Term Care of Older People* (Leveson Paper No. 3), (Solihull: The Leveson Centre for the Study of Ageing, Spirituality and Social Policy, 2002)

Johnson, Malcolm & Walker, Joanna, eds., *Spiritual Dimensions of Ageing* (Cambridge: Cambridge University Press, 2016)

Kidd, Sue Monk, *When the Heart Waits: Spiritual Direction for Life's Sacred Questions* (New York: Harper Collins, 2006)

Knox, Ian S., *Older People and the Church* (Edinburgh: T. & T Clark, 2002)

Kroll, Una, *Living Life to the Full: A Guide to Spiritual Health in Later Years* (London & New York: Continuum, 2006)

Kroll, Una, *The Humour of Old Age* (Leveson Paper No. 17), (Solihull: The Leveson Centre for the Study of Ageing, Spirituality and Social Policy, 2007)

Kushner, Harold S., *When bad things happen to good people* (London: Pan, 1981)

Kushner, Harold S., *When all you've ever wanted isn't enough* (London: Pan, 1987)

Lewin, Ann, *Watching for the Kingfisher* (Peterborough: Inspire, 2004)

Lively, Penelope, *Ammonites and Leaping Fish: A Life in Time* (London: Penguin, 2014)

Lomax, Eric, *The Railway Man* (London: Jonathan Cape, 1995)

Macdonald, Helen, *H is for Hawk* (London: Jonathan Cape, 2014)

MacKinlay, Elizabeth, *The Spiritual Dimension of Ageing* (London: Jessica Kingsley, 2001)

Mayne, Michael, *The Enduring Melody,* (London: Darton, Longman & Todd, 2006)

Mayne, Michael, *Dust that Dreams of Glory: Reflections on Lent and Holy Week* (Norwich: Canterbury Press, 2017)

McCrum, Robert, *Every Third Thought: On Life, Death and the Endgame* (London: Picador, 2017)

Merchant, Rob, *Pioneering the Third Age: The Church in an Ageing Population* (Carlisle: Paternoster Press, 2003)

Methodist Church and Church of England, *Seasons of My Soul: Conversations in the Second Half of Life* (London: Methodist Publishing, 2014)

Millar, Peter, *Finding Hope Again: Journeying through Sorrow and Beyond* (Norwich: Canterbury Press, 2003)

Miller, Jane, *Crazy Age: Thoughts on Being Old* (London: Virago, 2010)

Missinne, Leo, *Journeying through Old Age and Illness* (Leveson Paper No. 10), (Solihull: The Leveson Centre for the Study of Ageing, Spirituality and Social Policy, 2004)

Morisy, Ann, *Borrowing from the Future: A Faith-Based Approach to Intergenerational Equity* (London & New York: Continuum, 2011)

Morley, Janet, *The Heart's Time: A Poem a Day for Lent and Easter* (London: SPCK, 2011)

Mowat, Harriet & Donald, *The Freedom of Years: Ageing in Perspective* (Abingdon: The Bible Reading Fellowship, 2018)

Mursell, Gordon, *English Spirituality (Volume 1: From Earliest Times to 1700 & Volume 2: From 1700 to the Present Day)* (London: SPCK, 2001)

Neuberger, Julia, *The End or Merely the Beginning* (London: Counsel and Care, The Graham Lecture, 1995)

Nouwen, Henri, *Adam: God's Beloved* (London: Darton, Longman & Todd, 1997)

Nouwen, Henri, *Our Greatest Gift: A Meditation on Dying and Caring* (London: Hodder & Stoughton, 2002)

Oakley, Mark, *The Splash of Words: Believing in Poetry* (Norwich: Canterbury Press, 2016)

O'Donohue, John, *Benedictus: A Book of Blessings* (London: Bantam Press, 2007)

Reddie, Anthony G., *Faith, Stories and the Experience of Black Elders: Singing the Lord's Song in a Strange Land* (London: Jessica Kingsley, 2001)

Reid, Christopher, *A Scattering* (Oxford: Areté, 2009)

Robinson, Marilynne, *Gilead* (London, Virago, 2004)

Rohr OFM, Richard, *Falling Upward: A Spirituality for the Two Halves of Life* (London: SPCK, 2012)

Rush, Christopher, *To Travel Hopefully: Journal of a Death not Foretold* (London: Profile Books, 2006)

Sachs, Jonathan, *Celebrating Life: Finding Happiness in Unexpected Places* (London: Fount, 2000)

Santer, Mark, *Valuing Age: An Agenda for Society and Church* (Leveson Paper No. 2), (Solihull: The Leveson Centre for the Study of Ageing, Spirituality and Social Policy, 2001)

Scott, David, *Beyond the Drift: New & Selected Poems* (Hexham: Bloodaxe Books, 2014)

Scott-Maxwell, *Florida, The Measure of My Days* (London: Penguin, 1979)

Shamy, Eileen, *A Guide to the Spiritual Dimension of Care for People with Alzheimer's Disease and Related Dementia: More than Body, Brain and Breath* (London: Jessica Kingsley, 2003)

Snowdon, David, *Aging with Grace: The Nun Study and the Science of Old Age* (London: Fourth Estate, 2001)

Swinton, John, *Dementia: Living in the Memories of God* (Grand Rapids, Michigan: William B. Eerdmans, 2012)

Thane, Pat, ed., *The Long History of Old Age* (London: Thames & Hudson, 2005)

Thomas, R. S., *Collected Poems 1945-1990* (London: Phoenix, 2001)

Thomas, R. S., *Collected Later Poems 1988-2000* (Hexham: Bloodaxe, 2004)

Vanier, Jean, *Becoming Human* (London: Darton, Longman & Todd, 1999)

Vanstone, W. H., *The Stature of Waiting* (London: Darton, Longman & Todd, 1982)

Wainwright, David, *Being rather than Doing*, (Derby: Christian Council on Ageing, Occasional Paper No. 13, 2001)

Ware, Bronnie, *The Top Five Regrets of the Dying: A Life Transformed by the Dearly Departing* (London: Hay House: 2011)

Wilkinson, Alan, *One Foot in Eden* (Mirfield: Mirfield Publications, 2011)

Williams Rowan, *The Gifts Reserved for Age: Perceptions of the Elderly*, Lecture to mark the Centenary of Friends of the Elderly, Church House, Westminster (2005) www.archbishopofcanterbury.org/.../ archbishop-elderly-deserve-protection

Winter, David, *At the End of the Day: Enjoying Life in the Departure Lounge* (Abingdon: The Bible Reading Fellowship, 2013)

Woodward, James, *Befriending Death* (London: SPCK, 2005)

Woodward, James, *Valuing Age: Pastoral Ministry with Older People* (London: SPCK, 2008)

Woodward, James, (ed.), *Between Remembering and Forgetting: The Spiritual Dimensions of Dementia* (London: Mowbray, 2010)

Wordsworth, William, *The Poetical Works* (London: Frederick Warne, 1880)

NOTES

PREFACE

[1] For the modern charity see stjohnswinchester.co.uk/ and for its history see John Steel, *Nine Centuries of Care: A History of St. John's Winchester Charity* (Winchester: Sarsen Press, 2016) and Barbara Carpenter Turner, *St. John's Winchester Charity* (Chichester: Phillimore, 1992).

[2] See Ann Trueblood Raper & Anne C. Kalicki eds., *National Continuing Care Directory* (Washington: American Association of Homes for the Aging, 1988) p. 3

[3] Malcom Johnson, 'Spirituality, Biographical Review and Biographical Pain at the End of Life in Old Age', Malcolm Johnson & Joanna Walker (eds.), *Spiritual Dimensions of Ageing* (Cambridge: Cambridge University Press, 2016) p. 204.

[4] Janet Morley, *The Heart's Time: A Poem a Day for Lent and Easter* (London: SPCK, 2011) p. x.

[5] See Michelle de Kretser, *The Lost Dog* (London: Vintage, 2009) p. 46.

INTRODUCTION

[1] For life expectancy see www.ons.gov.uk > lifeexpectancies > bulletins > nation, and for those interested in the statistics on ageing Age UK's annual factsheet is always very informative. See www.ageuk.org.uk/Documents/EN-GB/Factsheets/Later_Life_uk_Factsheet.pdf.

[2] Ian S. Knox, *Older People and the Church* (Edinburgh: T. & T. Clark, 2002) p. 25.

[3] Miriam Margolyes interviewed by Donna Fergusson, *No one tells you what old age is like*, The Observer 29th January 2017.

[4] Genesis 5:27.

[5] Genesis 47:9.

[6] Marilynne Robinson, *Gilead* (London: Virago, 2004) p. 270.

[7] Psalm 37:25.

[8] David Snowdon, *Aging with Grace: The Nun Study and the Science of Old Age* (London: Fourth Estate, 2001) p. 9.

[9] William Shakespeare, *As You Like It*, Act 2 Scene 7.

[10] Pat Thane (ed.), *The Long History of Old Age* (London: Thames & Hudson, 2005) p. 300.

[11] See https://kalliope.org/en/text/lawrence2001061116 (accessed 5th June 2017).

[12] John Moses, *Divine Discontent: The Prophetic Voice of Thomas Merton* (London: Bloomsbury, 2014) p. 3.

[13] Jane Austen, *Emma* (London: Folio Society, 1975) p. 12.

[14] N. S. T. Thayer quoted in Elizabeth MacKinlay, *The Spiritual Dimension of Ageing* (London: Jessica Kingsley, 2001) p. 48.

[15] Gordon Mursell, *English Spirituality: From Earliest Times to 1700* (London: SPCK, 2008) p. 5.

[16] Ibid., p. 8.

[17] Quoted in Rob Merchant, *Pioneering the Third Age* (Carlisle: Paternoster Press, 2003) p. 126.

[18] Larry Culliford, 'Spirituality and Clinical Care', *British Medical Journal* (2002) Volume 325: 1434.

[19] See Mark Oakley, *The Splash of Words: Believing in Poetry*, (Norwich: Canterbury Press, 2016) p. 91.

[20] See Jonathan Sachs, *Celebrating Life: Finding Happiness in Unexpected Places* (London: Fount, 2000) p. 164.

[21] See Rosalie Hudson, 'Disembodied Souls or Soul-less bodies: Spirituality as Fragmentation', *Journal of Religion, Spirituality & Aging* (2006) 18 (2-3) p. 45.

[22] John O'Donohue, 'Spirituality as the Art of Presence', *The Way* Supplement (London: Burns & Oates, 1998), p. 100. See www.the way.org.uk/back/s092ODonohue.pdf (accessed 15th September 2018).

[23] Carole Bailey Stoneking, 'Modernity: The Social Construction of Aging', Stanley Hauerwas et al. eds., *Growing Old In Christ* (Grand Rapids: William B. Eerdmans, 2003) p. 67.

[24] Michael Mayne, *The Enduring Melody* (London: Darton Longman & Todd, 2006) p. 3.

[25] See Michael Lowis et al., 'The Role of Religion in mediating the Transfer to Residential Care', *Journal of Aging Studies* (2005) 19 pp. 349-362 and Michael Lowis et al., 'Religious and Secular Coping Methods used by Older Adults: An Empirical Investigation', *Journal of Religion, Spirituality & Aging* (2011) 23(4) pp. 279-303.

[26] Anthony Trollope, *Barchester Towers* (London: Blackie & Son, 1857) p. 89.

[27] See Rowan Williams, *The Gifts Reserved for Age: Perceptions of the Elderly*, 2005 Lecture to mark the centenary of Friends of the Elderly. Aoc2013brix.fatbeehive.com/articles.php/1518/archbishop-elderly-deserve-protection (accessed 3rd May 2018).

[28] Margaret Guenther, *Towards Holy Ground: Spiritual Direction in the Second Half of Life* (London: Darton Longman & Todd, 1996) p. 54.

[29] Ibid. p. 134.

[30] For more information on Anna Chaplaincy see https://www.annachaplaicy.org.uk/.

[31] James Woodward, *Valuing Age: Pastoral Ministry with Older People* (London: SPCK, 2008) p. 206.

[32] W. B. Yeats, 'Sailing to Byzantium', *Collected Poems* (Ware: Wordsworth editions, 2008) p. 164. Yeats is not the only poet to explore this. It has been said of Edward Thomas' poems that 'they are intent on inhabiting the moment across the full range of tenses the *is*, the *was* and the *will be*'. See Patrick McGuiness quoted in Richard Harries, H*aunted by Christ: Modern Writers and the Struggle for Faith* (London: SPCK, 2018) p. 56.

CHAPTER 1

[1] Monique Roffey, *The White Woman on the Green Bicycle* (London: Simon & Schuster, 2009) p. 271.

[2] Neil Ansell, *The Last Wilderness: A Journey into Silence* (London: Tinder Press) p. 61.

[3] St. Augustine, *Confessions,* tr. F. J. Sheed, (London: Sheed & Ward) Book 10 Chapter VIII p. 172.

[4] Quoted in Ann Morisy, *Borrowing from the Future: A Faith-based Approach to Intergenerational Equity* (London: Continuum, 2011) p. 142.

[5] Charlotte Brontë, *The Professor* (Ware: Wordsworth Classics, 1994) p. 193.

[6] Metropolitan Anthony of Sourozh, *The Spirituality of Old Age* (Derby: Christian Council on Ageing, Occasional Paper 4, 1993) p. 1.

[7] Jackie Treetops, 'The Memory Box', Albert Jewell (ed.), *Spirituality and Ageing* (London: Jessica Kingsley, 1999) p. 86.

[8] Viktor E. Frankl, *Man's Search for Meaning* (New York: Washington Square Press, 1985) p. 175.

[9] Carole Bailey Stoneking, 'Modernity: The Social Construction of Aging', Stanley Hauerwas et al. (eds.), *Growing Old in Christ,* op. cit. p. 83.

[10] Peter H. Millard and Chris S. Smith, 'Personal Belongings – A Positive Effect?' *The Gerontologist* (1981) 21(1).

[11] See ww.alicechilton.com/news/crabbit-old-woman for the poem and its background (accessed 17th June 2019).

[12] For those wanting to explore the use of a labyrinth in this way I recommend Sally Welch, *Walking the Labyrinth: A Spiritual and Practical Guide* (Norwich: Canterbury Press, 2010).

[13] For the poem and different authorship attributions see www.wowzone.com/fprints.htm (accessed 17th July 2019).

[14] Samuel Taylor Coleridge, *Table Talk* 18th December 1831. See https://archive.org/stream/cu31924105501633/cu31924105501633_djvu.txt (accessed 4th May 2018).

[15] Penelope Lively, *Ammonites and Leaping Fish: A Life in Time* (London: Penguin, 2014) p. 48.

[16] Joan Chittister OSB, *The Gift of Years: Growing Older Gracefully* (London: Darton, Longman & Todd, 2008) p. 3.

[17] Robert McCrum, *Every Third Thought: On Life, Death and the Endgame* (London: Picador, 2017) p. 36.

[18] William Wordsworth, 'Ode on Imitations of Immortality from Recollections of Early Childhood', The Poetical Works (London: Frederick Warne, 1880) p. 317

[19] Ann Morisy, *Borrowing from the Future,* op. cit., p. 195.

[20] Christie Watson, *Tiny Songbirds Far Away* (London: Quercus, 2011).

[21] Useful insights can be found in Yasmin Gunaratnam, *Death and the Migrant: Bodies, Borders and Care,* (London: Bloomsbury, 2013) and Anthony G. Reddie, *Faith, Stories and the Experience of Black Elders: Singing the Lord's Song in a Strange Land,* (London: Jessica Kingsley, 2001).

[22] Luke 1:6.

[23] Proverbs 20:29.

[24] Luke 2:25-38.

[25] T. S. Eliot, 'East Coker', *Collected Poems 1909-1962* (London: Faber & Faber, 1974) p. 191.

CHAPTER 2

1 Father George Congreve quoted in Ronald Blythe, *The View in Winter* (London: Penguin, 1981) p. 288.

2 William Wordsworth, 'The Solitary Reaper', *The Poetical Works* op. cit., p. 149.

3 Dannie Abse, *The Presence* (London: Hutchinson, 2007) p. 227.

4 Wendy Cope, 'The Widow', *Family Values* (London: Faber & Faber, 2011) p. 57.

5 Sebastian Barry, *Annie Dunne* (London: Faber & Faber, 2002) p. 25.

6 Thomas Hardy, *The Trumpet Major* (London: The Folio Society, 1990) p. 130

7 From his autobiography 'My Last Breath' quoted in John Swinton, *Dementia: Living in the Memories of God* (Grand Rapids: William B. Eerdmans, 2012) p. 190.

8 Samantha Harvey , *The Wilderness,* (London: Vintage, 2010).

9 Pádraig J. Daly, 'Alzheimers', *Clinging to the Myth,* (Dublin: Dedalus, 2007) p. 69.

10 Paul Higgs, 'New Cultures of Ageing: The Impact of the Third Age on Issues of Spirituality and Religion', Malcolm Johnson & Joanna Walker (eds.), *Spiritual Dimensions of Ageing* op. cit., p. 104.

11 Quoted in Michael Mayne, *The Enduring Melody* op. cit. p. 25.

12 Florida Scott-Maxwell, *The Measure of My Days* (London: Penguin, 1979). p. 42.

13 Helen Macdonald, *H is for Hawk* (London: Jonathan Cape, 2014) p. 171.

14 Dannie Abse, 'After the Memorial', *Two for Joy: Scenes from Married Life* (London: Hutchinson, 2010) p. 56.

15 Dannie Abse, 'Lachrymae', *The Presence* op. cit., p. 238.

16 Christopher Rush, *To Travel Hopefully: Journal of a Death not Foretold* (London: Profile Books, 2006).

17 William Shakespeare, *Macbeth*, Act 4 Scene 3.

18 Sheila Cassidy, *Sharing the Darkness: the Spirituality of Caring* (London: Darton, Longman & Todd, 1988) p. 5.

19 Sheila Cassidy, *Audacity to Believe* (London: Darton, Longman & Todd, 1992) p. 115.

20 Alfred Lord Tennyson, 'In Memoriam', *The Works of Alfred Lord Tennyson* (London: Macmillan, 1894) p. 247.

21 Galatians 6:2.

22 Jean-Pierre de Caussade (Kitty Muggeridge tr.), *The Sacrament of the Present Moment,* (New York: Harper Collins, 1989) p. 37.

23 Richard Rohr OFM, *Falling Upward: A Spirituality for the Two Halves of Life* (London: SPCK, 2012).

24 Ibid. p. 138.

25 John Steinbeck, *The Grapes of Wrath* (London: Penguin, 1951) p. 69.

26 Quoted in Peter Millar, *Finding Hope Again: Journeying through Sorrow and Beyond* (Norwich: Canterbury Press, 2003) p. 151.

CHAPTER 3

1 L. P. Hartley, The Go-Between, (London: Penguin, 1971).

2 Kazuo Ishiguro, *When We Were Orphans* (London: Faber & Faber, 2000) p. 277.

3 Malcolm Johnson, *Committed to the Asylum? The Long Term Care of Older People* (Leveson Paper No. 3), (Solihull: The Leveson Centre for the Study of Ageing, Spirituality and Social Policy, 2002). NB The author has subsequently expanded on this in subsequent publications.

4 See Richard Holloway, *Waiting for the Last Bus: Reflections on Life and Dying* (Edinburgh: Canongate, 2018) p. 52.

5 Archbishop Justin Welby interviewed by Harriet Sherwood in The Guardian 19th May 2018.

6 Eric Lomax, *The Railway Man* (London: Jonathan Cape, 1995).

7 A similar account of a prisoner of the Japanese finding reconciliation, on this occasion in a vision experienced at the Julian Cell in Norwich, is told by the former Chaplain of the Julian Shrine. See Robert Llewelyn, *With Pity Not With Blame: The Spirituality of Julian of Norwich and the Cloud of Unknowing for Today* (London: Darton, Longman & Todd, 1982) p. 1.

8 Mitch Albom, *Tuesdays with Morrie: An old man, a young man, and life's greatest lesson* (London: Time Warner, 1988) p. 167.

9 *The Straight Story* (1999) directed by David Lynch with screenplay by Mary Sweeney and John E. Roach.

[10] www.quotes.net > movies > straight_story_11029 (accessed 26th April 2020).

[11] Charles Dickens, *Oliver Twist* (London: Cassell, 1900) p. 197.

[12] Quoted in M. Therese Lysaught, 'Memory, Funerals, and the Communion of Saints: Growing Old and Practices of Remembering', Stanley Haurewas et al. (eds.), *Growing Old in Christ* op. cit., p. 290.

[13] Metropolitan Anthony of Sourozh, *The Spirituality of Age* op. cit., p. 3.

[14] Mary C. Grey, *To Rwanda and Back: Liberation Spirituality and Reconciliation* (London: Darton Longman & Todd, 2007) p. 45.

[15] See Matthew 22:37-40 and Mark 12:29-31.

[16] For a history of this see Ben Shephard, *After Daybreak: The Liberation of Belsen 1945* (London: Jonathan Cape, 2005) and for a more personal testimony Michael John Hargrave, *Bergen-Belsen 1945: A Medical Student's Journal* (London: Imperial College Press, 2014). A contemporaneous account was published in the British Medical Journal. See *Br Med J* 1945; 1 doi: https://doi.org/10.1136/bmj.1.4407.883-a (published 23 June 1945).

[17] Edith Eger, *The Choice* (London: Rider, 2017) p. 175.

[18] Jonathan Wittenberg, *Things my Dog has Taught Me : About being a better human* (London: Hodder & Stoughton, 2017) p. 130.

[19] Edith Eger, *The Choice* op. cit., p. 280.

[20] Rowan Williams quoted in Anne Long, *Approaches to Spiritual Direction* (Cambridge: Grove, 1984) p. 22.

[21] Sebastian Barry, *On Canaan's Side* (London: Faber & Faber, 2011) p. 217.

[22] Quoted in Richard Hoggart, *Promises to Keep: Thoughts in Old Age* (London: Continuum, 2005) p. 125.

[23] Luke 23:34.

[24] Pádraig J. Daly, 'Final Letter to Elizabeth', *The Lost Dreamers: New and Selected Poems* (Dublin: Dedalus Press, 1999) p. 15.

[25] Mary C. Grey, *To Rwanda and Back* op. cit., p. 37.

CHAPTER 4

[1] Charles Dickens, *The Pickwick Papers* (London: Cassell, 1900), p. 616.

[2] Michael Farrell, *Thy Tears Might Cease* (London: Hutchinson, 1963) p. 62.

[3] Quoted in Jonathan Sachs, *Celebrating Life* op. cit., p. 42.

[4] James Woodward, *Valuing Age* op. cit., p. 192.

[5] Ann Morisy, *Borrowing from the Future* op. cit., p. 90.

[6] Philip Larkin, 'Church Going', *Collected Poems* (London: Faber & Faber, 2003) p. 59.

[7] Margaret Guenther, *Holy Listening: The Art of Spiritual Direction* (London: Darton, Longman & Hall, 1992) p. ix.

[8] Quoted in Ian S. Knox, *Older People and the Church* op. cit., p. 49.

[9] Ann Lewin, 'Senior Moment', *Watching for the Kingfisher* (Peterborough: Inspire, 2004) p. 46.

[10] www.quotes.net > movies > straight_story_11029 (accessed 26th April 2020).

[11] Quoted in Sue Monk Kidd, *When the Heart Waits: Spiritual Direction for Life's Sacred Questions* (New York: Harper One, 2006) p. 159.

[12] See Jean Vanier, *Becoming Human* (London: Darton Longman & Todd, 1999) p. 127.

[13] Janet Morley, *The Heart's Time* op. cit., p. xi.

[14] Job 12:12.

[15] James 3:13.

[16] George Congreve SSJE, *Treasures of Hope for the Evening of Life* (London: Longmans, Green & Co, 1920) p. 161.

[17] Ronald Blythe, *The View in Winter* op. cit., p. 249.

CHAPTER 5

[1] J. Lynn & D. M. Adamson quoted in Malcolm Johnson, 'Spirituality, Biographical Review and Biographical Pain atthe End of Life in old Age', Malcolm Johnson & Joanna Walker (eds.), *Spiritual Dimensions of Ageing* op. cit. p. 201.

[2] Quoted in James Woodward, *Valuing Age* op. cit., p. 74.

[3] Richard Rohr, *Falling Upward* op. cit., p. x.

[4] Sue Monk Kidd, *When the Heart Waits* op. cit., p. 57.

[5] Timothy Radcliffe OP, *Alive in God: A Christian Imagination* (London: Bloomsbury Continuum, 2019) p. 105.

[6] Ibid. p. 94

[7] Circular letter to friends September 1968 quoted in Jim Forest , *Living with Wisdom: A Life of Thomas Merton* (New York: Orbis, 1991) p. 220.

[8] Ann Lewin, *Watching for the Kingfisher* op. cit. p. v.

[9] Jeffrey Harris, 'Believing', Albert Jewell (ed.), *Older People and the Church* (Peterborough: Methodist Publishing House, 2001) p. 96.

[10] The Methodist Church & The Church of England, *Seasons of My Soul: Conversations in the Second Half of Life*, (London: Methodist Publishing, 2014). This explores many of the themes covered in this book over eight sessions with helpful discussion material.

[11] Margaret Guenther, *Holy Listening* op. cit., p. 97.

[12] St. Augustine, *Confessions* op. cit., p.188.

[13] George Herbert, 'The Flower', *Selected Poems* (London: Bloomsbury, 1997) p .83.

[14] Kathleen Jamie, 'The Wishing Tree' in *The Tree House* (Picador Poetry, 2004) quoted in Kirsten McKenzie, *The Chapel at the Edge of the World* (London: John Murray, 2009) p. 1.

[15] John 15:1-4.

[16] Quoted in Wayne Booth (ed.), *The Art of Growing Older: Writers on Living and Aging* (Chicago: University of Chicago Press, 1992) p. 291.

[17] Helen Dunmore, 'My life's stem was cut', *Inside the Wave* (Hexham: Bloodaxe Books, 2017) p. 23

CHAPTER 6

[1] Jonathan Sachs, *Celebrating Life* op. cit., p. 12.

[2] Graham Greene, *The Human Factor* (London: Bodley Head, 1978) p. 187.

[3] Kamila Shamsie, *Burnt Shadows* (London: Bloomsbury, 2009) p. 131.

[4] Philippians 4:11-13.

[5] St. Mathew 6:23.

[6] Proverbs 17:22.

[7] Anne Brontë, *Agnes Grey* (London: Classics Book Club, 1954) p. 62.

[8] Ecclesiasticus 30:22.

[9] Ecclesiasticus 30:25.

[10] John Betjeman, 'The Last Laugh', *A Nip in the Air* (London: John Murray, 1974) p. 62.

[11] Umberto Eco, *The Name of the Rose* (London: Picador, 1984) p. 95.

[12] Sue Monk Kidd, *When the Heart Waits op. cit.,* p. 98.

[13] Chapter 6, Rule of St. Benedict.

[14] Harold S. Kushner, *When all you've ever wanted isn't enough* (London: Pan, 1986) p. 93.

[15] See Diarmaid MacCulloch, *A History of Christianity* (London: Allen Lane, 2009) p. 786.

[16] Jane Austen, *Emma* (London: Folio Society, 1975) p. 23.

[17] Kazuo Ishiguro, *The Remains of the Day* (London: Faber & Faber, 1989) p. 256.

[18] Florida Scott Maxwell, *The Measure of my Days* op. cit., p. 143.

[19] See George Eliot, *Silas Marner* (London: William Blackwood & Sons, 1890) p. 121.

[20] Psalm 36:7-9.

[21] John Carden (ed.), *A Procession of Prayers: Meditations and Prayers from Around the World*, (London: Cassell, 1998) p. 43.

CHAPTER 7

[1] Jane Austen, *Emma* (London: Folio Society, 1975) p. 74.

[2] Joan Chittister, *The Gift of Years* op. cit., p. 132.

[3] Susan A. Eisenhandler, 'Religion, Faith, Belief and Disbelief in Old Age', Malcolm Johnson & Joanna Walker eds., *Spiritual Dimensions of Ageing* op. cit., p. 172.

[4] See https://www.google.co.uk/amp/s/www.biography.com/.amp/news/henri-matisse-the-cut-outs-moma (accessed 22nd October 2019). I am grateful to my daughter Alice for sharing this with me.

[5] See Carol Kennedy, *A Pebble in the Pond: A Memoir in Prose and Verse* (Eastleigh: Millers Dale Publications, 2015)

[6] I Thessalonians 4:1.

[7] Ibid, 5:25.

[8] George Congreve, *Treasures of Hope for the Evening of Life* op. cit., p. 217.

[9] Ibid, p. 125.

[10] Alfred Tennyson, 'Ulysses', *The Works of Alfred Lord Tennyson* (London: Macmillan, 1894) p. 95.

[11] See Jane Millar, *Crazy Age: Thoughts on Being Old* (London: Virago, 2010) p. 132.

[12] See https://www.bath.ac.uk/.../how-old-peoples-home-for-4-year-olds-might-force-a-shak.., accessed 20th June 2019.

[13] See John O'Donohue *Anam Cara* quoted in Alan Hargrave, *Living Well: Finding a 'Rule of Life' to Revitalize and Sustain Us* (London: SPCK, 2010) p. 104.

[14] Mark Oakley, *The Splash of Words op. cit.,* p. xxvi.

[15] Etty Hillesum, *A Diary 1941-43* (London: Grafton Books, 1985) p. 50.

[16] Florida Scott-Maxwell, *The Measure of My Days* op. cit., p. 75.

[17] Thomas Merton, 'Great and Small', *Collected Poems* (New York: New Directions, 1980) p. 879.

CHAPTER 8

[1] Ruth 1:16-17.

[2] Marilynne Robinson, *Gilead* op. cit., p. 26.

[3] Gerard Manley Hopkins, 'The Wreck of the Deutschland', *Collected Poems* (Oxford: Oxford University Press, 1970) p. 53.

[4] Richard Llewellyn, *How Green Was My Valley* (Toronto: Ryerson Press, 1940) p. 451.

[5] George Congreve, *Treasures of Hope for the Evening of Life* op. cit., p.79.

[6] Jim Cotter, 'Humming and Patient Attentiveness' in John Wilkins (ed.) *How I Pray* (London: Darton, Longman & Todd, 1993) p. 31.

[7] Florida Scott-Maxwell, *The Measure of My Days* op. cit., p. 34.

[8] Mary Craig, *Blessings* (London: Hodder & Stoughton, 1979).

[9] Fyodor Dostoevsky, *The Brothers Karamazov* (London: Folio Society, 1964) p. 316.

[10] Richard Harries, *Haunted by Christ: Modern Writers and the Struggle for Faith* op. cit., p. xiv.

[11] W. H. Auden, 'As I Walked Out One Evening' in *As I Walked Out One Evening: Songs, Ballads, Lullabies, Limericks, and other Light Verse* (London: Faber & Faber, 1995) p. 59.

[12] Edwin Muir, *Collected Poems* (London: Faber & Faber, 1984) p. 227.

[13] Christopher Reid, *A Scattering* (London: Areté, 2009) p. 62.

[14] Genesis 12:2.

[15] See Matthew 5:1-12.

[16] George Eliot, *Daniel Deronda* (London: Penguin, 1967) p. 577.

[17] Proverbs 10:22.

[18] J. Philip Newell, *Each Day and Each Night: A Weekly Cycle of Prayers from Iona* (Glasgow: Wild Goose Publications, 1994) p. 52.

CHAPTER 9

[1] Raynor Winn, *The Salt Path* (London: Penguin, 2019) p.184.

[2] Ann Morisy, *Borrowing from the Future* op. cit., p. 167.

[3] 2 Corinthians 12:10.

[4] See www.sacred-texts.com/chr/seil78.htm Accessed 2nd April 2019.

[5] Gerard Manley Hopkins, 'Patience, hard thing!', *Poems* op. cit., p.102.

[6] See https://joansrome.worpress.com/.../resignation-is-not-a-christian-virtue-a-papal-plea-s, accessed 1st May 2018.

[7] Richard Holloway, *Waiting for the Last Bus* op. cit., p. 149.

[8] Henri Nouwen, *Our Greatest Gift: A Meditation on Dying and Caring* (London: Hodder & Stoughton, 2002) p. 56.

[9] Jean-Pierre De Causade, *The Sacrament of the Present Moment* op. cit., p. 62.

[10] Ibid, p.77.

[11] Jane Austen, *Persuasion,* (London: Folio Society, 1961) p. 145.

[12] Ibid.

[13] William Hazlitt, 'On Going on a Journey', *Essays* (London: Folio Society, 1964) p. 75.

[14] Dannie Abse, 'Last Visit of Uncle Isidore', *Speak Old Parrot,* (London: Hutchinson, 2013) p. 22. See also Dannie Abse, *The Presence* op. cit. p. 28.

[15] George Congreve, *Treasures of Hope for the Evening of Life* op. cit., p. 10.

[16] Ian S. Knox, *Older People and the Church* op. cit. p. 30.

[17] Metropolitan Anthony, *The Spirituality of Old Age* op. cit., p. 7.

[18] James Woodward, *Valuing Age* op. cit. p. 194.

[19] See Micah 6:8.

[20] Thomas Merton OCSO, *New Seeds of Contemplation* (New York: New Directions, 2007) p. 99.

[21] Sister Mary David OSB, *The Joy of God: Collected Writings* (London: Bloomsbury Continuum, 2019) p. 101.

[22] Patrick Gale, *A Perfectly Good Man* (London: Fourth Estate, 2012) p. 30.

[23] Robin Daniels, *The Virgin Eye: Towards a Contemplative View of Life* (Watford: Instant Apostle, 2016) p. 52.

[24] Pádraig J. Daly, 'Prayer in Age', *God in Winter*, (Dublin: Dedalus Press, 2015) p. 51

CHAPTER 10

[1] Timothy Radcliffe OP, *What is the point of being a Christian?* (London: Burns & Oates, 2005) p. 24.

[2] W. H. Vanstone, *The Stature of Waiting* (London: Darton, Longman & Todd, 1982) p.70.

[3] John 21:18.

[4] Florida Scott-Maxwell, *The Measure of my Days* op. cit., p. 17.

[5] John Milton, 'On His Blindness', Arthur Quiller-Couch (ed.), *The Oxford Book of English Verse 1250-1918 (*Oxford: OUP, 1939) p. 352.

[6] Quoted in Paul Murray OP, *Scars: Essays, Poems and Meditation on Affliction* (London: Bloomsbury, 2014) p.18

[7] Henri Nouwen, *Adam: God's Beloved* (London: Darton, Longman & Todd, 1997) p. 76.

[8] Ibid p. 77.

[9] Finuala Dowling, 'At eighty-five, my mother's mind', *Notes from the Dementia Ward* (Cape Town: Kwela Books, 2008) p. 7.

[10] Margaret Drabble, *The Dark Flood Rises* (Edinburgh: Canongate, 2016) p. 122.

[11] W. H. Vanstone, *The Stature of Waiting* op. cit. p. 70.

[12] Michael Mayne, *Dust that Dreams of Glory: Reflections on Lent and Holy Week* (Norwich: Canterbury Press, 2017) p. 75.

[13] Etty Hillesum, *A Diary 1941-43* op. cit., p. 217.

[14] 2 Corinthians 12: 9.

[15] Jonathan Sachs, *Celebrating Life* op. cit. p. 36.

[16] Quoted in Eric James, *A Life of John A. T. Robinson: Scholar, Pastor, Prophet* (London: Collins, 1987) p. 317.

CHAPTER 11

[1] Pádraig J. Daly, 'Minnie', *The Lost Dreamers: New and Selected Poems*, (Dublin: Dedalus, 1999) p. 116.

[2] John 19:30.

[3] John Vincent quoted in Paul Higgs, 'New Cultures of Ageing: The Impact of the Third Age on Issues of Spirituality and Religion', Malcolm Johnson & Joanna Walker, *Spiritual Dimensions of Ageing* op. cit. p.146

[4] Quoted in Robert McCrum, *Every Third Thought* op. cit., p. 138.

[5] From *Glory to thee, my God, this night,* Words: Thomas Ken & Music: Thomas Tallis.

[6] Harold S. Kushner, *When Bad Things Happen to Good People* (London: Pan, 1981) p. 155.

[7] Etty Hillesum, *A Diary 1941-43.* op. cit., *p.174.*

[8] Guenther, *Toward Holy Ground* op. cit., p.136.

[9] David Hein, *Geoffrey Fisher: Archbishop of Canterbury* (Cambridge: James Clarke & Co) p. 104.

[10] Anthony Trollope, *Barchester Towers* op. cit., p. 1 & 3.

[11] Genesis 45:28.

[12] Diarmaid MacCulloch, *A History of Christianity* op. cit., p. 1013.

[13] Atul Gawande, *Being Mortal: Illness, Medicine, and What Matters in the End* (London: Profile Books, 2014) p. 128.

[14] Rachel Clarke, *Dear Life: A doctor's story of love and loss* (London: Little, Brown, 2020) p. 101

[15] J. C. Van der Meer quoted in Willem Berger, *The Last Achievement* (London: Grail, 1974) p. 37.

[16] U. A. Fanthorpe, 'The Passing of Alfred', *Selected Poems* (London: Enitharmon Press, 2013) p. 32.

[17] John Cornwell, *Newman's Unquiet Grave: The Reluctant Saint* (London: Continuum, 2010) p. 226.

[18] W. H. Auden, 'A Lullaby', *Selected Poems* (London: Faber & Faber, 1979) p. 299.

[19] Bronnie Ware, *The Top Five Regrets of the Dying: A Life Transformed by the Dearly Departing* (London: Hay House, 2011).

[20] See Helen Gardner (ed.), *The New Oxford Book of English Verse* (Oxford: Clarendon Press, 1972) p. 942.

[21] William Shakespeare, *King Lear,* Act 5 Scene 3.

[22] Recollections of Bishop Wilkinson of St. Andrew's quoted in George Congreve, *Treasures of Hope* op. cit., p. 204.

[23] Romans 2:7.

CHAPTER 12

[1] Quoted in Albert Jewell (ed.), *Older People and the Church* (Peterborough: Methodist Publishing House, 2001) p. 95.

[2] John Donne (H. W. Garrod ed.), *Poetry & Prose* (Oxford: Clarendon Press, 1946) p. 66.

[3] John 14:2.

[4] Richard Hoggart, *Promises to Keep: Thoughts in Old Age* op. cit., p. 139.

[5] David Snowden, *Aging with Grace* op. cit., p. 3.

[6] Carole Bailey Stoneking, "Modernity: The Social Construction of Aging", Stanley Hauerwas et al (eds.), *Growing Older in Christ* op. cit., p.74.

[7] Quoted in Michael Mayne, *Pray, Love, Remember* (London: Darton Longman & Todd, 1998) p. 128.

[8] Emily Dickinson (Thomas H. Johnson ed.), *The Complete Poems* (London: Faber & Faber, 2016), p. 334.

[9] Elizabeth Jennings (Emma Mason ed.), 'Rembrandt's Late Self-Portraits', *Collected Poems*, (Manchester: Carcanet Press, 2012) p. 324

[10] R. S. Thomas, 'The Echoes Return Slow', *Collected Later Poems 1988-2000* (Hexham: Bloodaxe Books, 2004) p. 72

[11] 1 Corinthians 13:8.

[12] 1 John 4:16b.

[13] Quoted in Patrick Hart and Jonathan Montaldo (eds.), *The Intimate Merton: His Life from His Journals Thomas Merton* (Oxford: Lion, 2000) p. 86.

[14] John Austin Baker, *The Foolishness of God* (London: Darton, Longman & Todd, 1970) p. 406.

[15] George Congreve, *Treasures of Hope* op. cit. p. 205.

[16] For discussion of authorship see www.theworshipbook.com/blog/lyrics-whodunnit, accessed 2nd May 2018. Corrie Ten Bloom does use an embroidery simile in the autobiographical account of her imprisonment in Ravensbruck Nazi concentration camp: 'Everything looks like a confused piece of embroidery work, meaningless and ugly. But that is the underside. Some day we shall see the right side and shall be amazed and thankful.' See Corrie Ten Bloom, *A Prisoner and Yet...* (London: Christian Literature Crusade, 1954) p. 74

[17] Ann Lewin, 'Celtic Knot', *Watching for the Kingfisher* op. cit. p.120.

[18] See Philip Hoare, *Leviathan, or The Whale* (London: Fourth Estate, 2009) p.195.

[19] Charles Pinches, 'The Virtues of Aging', Stanley Hauerwas et al (eds.), *Growing Old in Christ* op. cit., p. 224.

[20] John 6:12.

[21] Alan Wilkinson, *One Foot in Eden* (Mirfield: Mirfield Publications, 2008) p. 131.

[22] David Scott, 'Resurrection', *Beyond the Drift: New and Selected Poems* (Hexham: Bloodaxe Books, 2014) p. 188.

[23] Robin Daniels, *The Virgin Eye* op. cit., p.176.

ACKNOWLEDGEMENTS

The author and publisher are grateful for permission to reprint extracts from the following:

'Lachrymae' from *The Presence'* by Dannie Abse published by Hutchinson (2007). ©2007 published by Hutchinson. Reproduced by permission of The Random House Group Ltd.

'After the Memorial' from *Two for Joy: Scenes from Married Life* by Dannie Abse published by Hutchinson (2010). ©2010 published by Hutchinson. Reproduced by permission of The Random House Group Ltd.

'Last Visit of Uncle Isidore' from *Speak Old Parrot* by Dannie Abse published by Hutchinson (2013). ©2013 published by Hutchinson. Reproduced by permission of The Random House Group Ltd.

'As I walked out one evening' from *As I walked out one evening: Songs, Ballads, Lullabies, Limericks, and other Light Verse* by W. H. Auden published by Faber &Faber (1995) and 'A Lullaby' from *Selected Poems* by W. H. Auden published by Faber & Faber (1979) copyright © 1969, 1969, by W. H. Auden, renewed. Reprinted by permission of Curtis Brown Limited.

Annie Dunne by Sebastian Barry published by Faber & Faber (2002). *On Canaan's Side* by Sebastian Barry published by Faber & Faber (2011). 'The Last Laugh' from *A Nip in the Air* by John Betjeman published by John Murray (1974). © 1974 John Betjeman. Reproduced by permission of John Murray Publishers, an imprint of Hodder and Stoughton Limited.

'The Widow' from 'Family Values' by Wendy Cope published by Faber & Faber (2011).

'Final Letter to Elizabeth' and 'Minnie' from *The Last Dreamers: New and Selected Poems* by Pádraig J. Daly published by Dedalus Press (1999). www.dedaluspress.com

'Alzheimer's' from *Clinging to the Myth* by Pádraig J. Daly published by Dedalus Press (2007). www.dedaluspress.com

'Prayer in Age' from *God in Winter* by Pádraig J. Daly published by Dedalus Press (2015). www.dedaluspress.com

'The love a life can show below' from *The Poems of Emily Dickinson: Reading*

'At eighty-five, my mother's mind' from *Notes from the Dementia Ward* by Finuala Dowling published by Kwela Books (2008).

'My life's stem was cut' from *Inside the Wave* by Helen Dunmore published by Bloodaxe Books (2017).

'East Coker' from *Collected Poems 1909-1962* by T. S. Eliot published by Faber & Faber (1974).

'The Passing of Alfred' from *Selected Poems* by U. A. Fanthorpe published by Enitharmon Press (2013).

The Remains of the Day by Kazuo Ishiguro published by Faber & Faber (1989).

When We Were Orphans by Kazuo Ishiguro published by Faber & Faber (2000).

'The Wishing Tree' from *The Tree House* by Kathleen Jamie published by Picador Poetry (2004). Used by permission of Pan Macmillan.

'Rembrandt's Late Self-Portraits' from *Collected Poems* by Elizabeth Jennings published by Carcanet Press (2012). Used by permission of David Higham Associates Limited.

'Celtic Knot' from *Watching for the Kingfisher* by Ann Lewin which is © Ann Lewin, 2004, 2006 and 2009. Published by Canterbury Press. Used by permission. rights@hymnsam.co.uk

'Senior Moments' from *Watching for the Kingfisher* by Ann Lewin which is © Ann Lewin, 2004, 2006 and 2009. Published by Canterbury Press. Used by permission. rights@hymnsam.co.uk

'Great and Small' from *The Way of Chuang Tzu* by Thomas Merton, copyright ©1965 by The Abbey of Gethsemani. Reprinted by permission of New Directions Publishing Corp.

'One Foot in Eden' from *Collected Poems* by Edwin Muir published by Faber & Faber (1984).

'Lucinda's Way' from *A Scattering* by Christopher Reid. Published by

Areté Books, 2009. Copyright © Christopher Reid. Reproduced by permission of the author c/o Rogers, Coleridge & White Ltd., 20 Powis Mews, London W11 1JN.

The White Woman on the Green Bicycle by Monique Roffey published by Simon & Schuster (2009).

'The Echoes Return Slow' from *Collected Later Poems 1988-2000* by R.S. Thomas published by Bloodaxe Books (2004).

'Resurrection' from *Beyond the Drift: New & Selected Poems* by David Scott published by Bloodaxe Books (2014).

Burnt Shadows by Kamila Shamsie published by Bloomsbury (2009).

One Foot in Eden by Alan Wilkinson published by Mirfield Publications (2011).

Every effort has been made to obtain permissions for extracts from copyright material. The publisher apologises for any omissions and would be happy to rectify these in further reprints.

Printed in Great Britain
by Amazon

78328165R00088